Marketing for Small Publishers

MARKETING for SMALL PUBLISHERS
Bill Godber, Robert Webb and Keith Smith

Foreword by TIM WATERSTONE

journeyman

LONDON • BOULDER, COLORADO

This edition first published 1992
by Journeyman Press
345 Archway Road, London N6 5AA
and 5500 Central Avenue,
Boulder, Colorado 80301, USA

First edition by Keith Smith published 1980 by
Inter-Action Trust Ltd, reprinted 1980, 1981 and 1983

This edition by Bill Godber and Robert Webb, based on the original
edition by Keith Smith.

British Library Cataloguing in Publication Data
A catalogue record for this book is available from the British Library

ISBN 1 85172 034 0 hb
ISBN 1 85172 035 9 pb

Designed and produced for Journeyman Press by
Chase Production Services, Chipping Norton
Typeset from authors' disks by Stanford Desktop Publishing Services
Printed in Finland by WSOY

Contents

v

Foreword
Tim Waterstone

Of course too many books are published in this market – 46,000 in 1981, 68,000 in 1991 and – who knows? – 90,000 in 2001.

But Britain does remain a market strangely underrated by those of us who make our living within it. The school textbook market has suffered in recent years through public spending cuts and a declining school population, but the trade market is perfectly resilient. The most recent figures show that the British (at £43 per head per annum) may spend less on books than the Germans (£57) or the Americans (£51), but are ahead of most others, including the French (£37) and the Dutch (£32).

Research on reading habits show the British book buyer in a perfectly adequate light. The Publishers Association Trade Year Book for 1992 shows data indicating that 55 per cent of people here in the UK read at least one book per month. Comparable figures show that only one third of the French read as much. Barely 20 per cent of Italians read as much as one book per quarter.

The British book trade does have an extraordinary capacity for self-criticism and despair. The numbers show a much more encouraging position than trade sentiment and rumour would suggest.

Particularly striking is the Year Book's conclusion that although – hardly unexpectedly – the financial performance of the industry has deteriorated somewhat over the last five years, publishers' return on capital employed is still higher than that of UK industry overall, just as it was ten years before.

We publish well in Britain and we booksell well. British bookshops are now perhaps as good as any in the world; heavy on inventory investment per square foot, and staffed by devoted and professional people.

The challenge for the small publisher is to make every penny of necessarily limited marketing budgets work. Without good marketing, the small list will fail, sadly irrespective of the quality of its product.

By good marketing I mean simply this. The publishers should package, price and design their titles with a clear focus on the targetted consumer. There must be a clear and total understanding of the way each of the target booksellers works, and sales management – a vital component of the marketing mix – must be geared to this.

Waterstone's have one requirement, Dillons another. We both require sensitive and demanding support from publishers' sales forces. It is *not* a question of trying to oversell us on frontlist. Waterstone's is overwhelmingly a backlist bookseller – backlist sales alone this trading year will be over £100 million – and what we require from publishers' salespeople is a sense of partnership, working with the branches on a sensible purchase programme of suitable frontlist titles, and reliably and speedily replenishing backlist inventory.

We need intelligent advice on our core stock lists, and swift and efficient dealing with queries and claims. We need authors to come to us and meet their public. What we do *not* need is heaps of dumpbins – they make a mess and they lead to overstocks – and hyped up over-selling of speculative print runs.

W H Smith, with their deeply rooted central buying system, have different criteria and different requirements. The independents – many of whom offer a quite essential regional facility – are as important to the small publisher as any of the rest of us.

There really is a healthy market out there for us all. The British buy books and they always will. But publishing has to be in the final analysis a marketing-led activity. No author and no book is so good that it will not be lost if the basic disciplines of pricing, design and focused and sophisticated sales management are not employed.

Good marketing – intelligent marketing – is more than necessary for small publishers: it is the key to survival. This wise book should be treated as required reading.

Timothy Waterstone
Chief Executive
Waterstone's Booksellers Limited

September 1992

Acknowledgements

The need for a guide to marketing for small publishers was originally formulated by members of Publishers Distribution Cooperative and the Radical Publishers Group in the late 1970s. Their support and guidance, and that of other publishers and distributors, was acknowledged by Keith Smith in the first edition of this book in 1980.

In addition to those mentioned below, therefore, the joint authors of this revised edition would like to reiterate their acknowledgements to the many people who made the original edition possible.

Those to whom we are jointly and individually indebted for support and advice and for help in the preparation of this edition are:

Larry Fisher and Adam Padamsee for their assistance in compiling the bibliography;
Colleagues at Turnaround Distribution;
Malcolm Smith of Karnac Books;
Martin Lee of W H Smith;
Colleagues at the Minority Rights Group;
Charles Gibbs of Prentice Hall International;
Ion Mills of Oldcastle Books;
Bill Norris of Central Books;
Trevor Fenwick of Euromonitor;
David Musson of Oxford University Press;
Kingsley Dawson of Bookspeed;
Jane Lawrence of Harcourt Brace Jovanovich;
Jane Brennan, Nick Coleman and Jane Goodsir for the use of computers;
Alison Clixby and Swati Patel both previously of Interchange Books;
Anne Beech and Roger Van Zwanenberg of Pluto Press.

Finally, thanks to Tim Waterstone for writing the Foreword.

Introduction

In 1991, over 60,000 books were published in the UK. By the end of the millennium, if current trends continue, the total will have reached 100,000 per annum. Sales of individual titles, however, are declining as publishers flood the market with more and more books.

The large publishing conglomerates are fighting to retain their share of this increasingly competitive market by mergers and takeovers, by attracting best-selling authors from their competitors with ever increasing advances and by spending more and more money on marketing their products. Such options, unhappily, are not available to the small- and medium-sized publishers whose success or failure relies on their ability to acquire potentially saleable titles and to market them creatively and effectively within limited budgets.

It seems unlikely that any book will teach a publisher how to commission best-selling titles, but many aspects of marketing can be learnt and it is hoped that this guide will assist in the process. Like Keith Smith, the author of the original edition, we have written it in the belief that publishing is unnecessarily mystified and can often be reduced to basic factors. Accordingly, we have concentrated our efforts on the practical aspects of marketing for publishers and have steered clear of devoting space to methods and techniques which are unlikely to have a general application. If, for example, you want your books sold effectively to booksellers, bought by public libraries or reviewed in the national press, then we hope that you should find much of the book of value.

Our definition of marketing is not limited simply to finding ways of selling the end product. In our view, the marketing process starts from the moment a manuscript is accepted for publication and ends only when it reaches its end user – the reader. Indeed, even then, it can play a part in encouraging the purchaser to buy another book. Marketing, therefore, can cover a wide range of activities, from choosing a book's title, designing an appropriate cover and circulating bibliographical details, through to alerting the book trade, the press and the public to its availability and ensuring that retailers and other suppliers can obtain it quickly and efficiently. In addition, we have provided a brief section on selling rights which we hope will provide a useful introduction to what is becoming an increasingly complex area.

The various marketing possibilities open to a book publisher can be derived from a consideration of the following flow diagram. This shows the primary distribution routes from a book's conception to the end user.

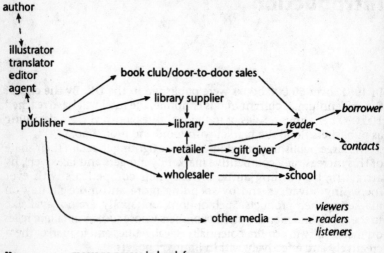

Key: ——————▶message passes in book form
     – – – –▶message passes in nonbook form
     italics indicate absorber of message

This book is addressed primarily to two groups of readers. First, to the small commercial publisher who it is hoped will find all sections of some relevance. Their marketing must seek to be as effective as that of major publishers with considerably larger resources and it is essential that they consider every avenue open to them if they are to compete successfully.

Secondly, it is addressed to publishers working within voluntary organisations and campaigning groups. Such publishing operations are not in business primarily to make money but in order to provide information or to spread a message. To do so their marketing must be as effective as that of any commercial publishing house, yet they usually have to achieve this with slimmer resources and often in an uninterested environment.

We hope it may also be of use to those in large publishing companies who wish to broaden or refresh their knowledge or who require a basic handbook for occasional reference. Large publishing houses will find it a useful resource in their training.

Every effort has been made to ensure that the information in this book is correct at 31 January 1992. Unless clearly stated in the text, the mention of a company, organisation, service or product does not constitute a recommendation.

1

Infrastructure of the UK Book Trade

Much of book marketing is a matter of knowing the resources available to a publisher and then putting them to work in an effective way. However, it is important to have an understanding of the infrastructure of the industry in which one is working and a broad overview of the market in which one has chosen to operate. In this opening chapter, we will look at the state of the UK book trade in the 1990s and consider recent developments in publishing and book retailing. No publisher can afford to run their business in isolation and some knowledge of the wider aspects of the publishing industry should help prepare even the smallest publisher for what may lie ahead as their business develops.

Since the first edition of this book was published in 1980, the UK publishing and bookselling industry has undergone substantial change. The 1980s heralded a period of takeovers and mergers and many of the companies mentioned in the original edition have since been bought and sold several times over. Others have changed their identity so much as to be virtually unrecognisable while some have simply vanished. Such was the confusion caused by these numerous changes of ownership that in March 1990, *The Bookseller* published a special 'Who Owns Whom' supplement in response to demands from the trade for some clarification.

Much of this metamorphosis stemmed from increased interest in the industry from the City which up until the 1980s had regarded publishing and bookselling, in general, as bad risks. This view underwent considerable revision during the decade as financial institutions began to recognise 'information' as a valuable commodity that was ripe for further development. Many publishers were seen to be underexploiting their valuable backlists, others were viewed as too small to maximise their profit potential. Booksellers, with a few exceptions, were in danger of stagnating whilst the 'retail revolution' – albeit shortlived – passed them by.

Nevertheless it is likely that other factors – for example the death of Robert Maxwell at the end of 1991 – will ensure that upheavals within the industry will continue well into the 1990s. However, we can take a brief look at some of the UK book trade's major components with reasonable confidence that many of them will still be around at the end of the decade.

Publishers

As might be expected, the major houses were the most active in gobbling up their smaller and less well-financed competitors.

HarperCollins appeared on the scene following the purchase of Collins by News International in early 1989 and then went on to buy Thorsons and Unwin Hyman amongst others. Earlier acquisitions by the group included Granada Publishing (renamed Grafton) and Bartholomew. Their wide variety of imprints also include the paperback lists – Flamingo, Fontana and Paladin.

Pearson also increased their share of the market under the Longman Group banner which includes Penguin Books. Acquisitions added Frederick Warne, Pitman Publishing, Michael Joseph and Hamish Hamilton to their numerous imprints.

Random Century was formed in mid-1988 after the purchase of Century Hutchinson by Random House Inc which had been created by the earlier purchase of Bodley Head, Cape and Chatto & Windus. Hutchinson, in 1985, had itself been purchased by Century.

Meanwhile, Reed International – owners of Butterworths – purchased Octopus thus adding Hamlyn, Heinemann and Mitchell Beazley to their lists. They followed this up with the acquisition of ABP's general list and George Philip.

Of course, change was not confined to the large conglomerates and many smaller organisations underwent considerable development during this period. Of particular interest are those companies which initially were seen as 'alternative' or 'radical' publishers but whose products are now generally recognised as part of the mainstream. Their publications not only created a new market for booksellers but influenced the publishing programmes of many larger houses which were only too eager to jump on the bandwagon.

Perhaps the most established of these is Virago, the pioneer feminist publisher which had been purchased – to the surprise of many – by the Chatto, Bodley Head & Cape group in 1982 but which re-established its independence with a management buyout in 1987 when the group was sold to Random House. Further evidence of the strength of women's publishing can be seen in the examples of the Women's Press, who introduced Alice Walker to a British audience, and Sheba whose mixture of books from black women, lesbians and working class women still continues to inspire.

Gay publishing too continues to flourish and, like feminist publishing, has significantly influenced the programmes of several major houses. The Gay Men's Press (now GMP) has been the leader in this field; prospering in a decade not overly sympathetic to gay issues.

Interest in Third World issues has been particularly well served by Zed Press whose success in a notoriously difficult area of publishing gives credit to their initiatives and enterprise. Saqi Books (formerly Al Saqi) have maintained their strong profile as specialist publishers of material relating to the politics and culture of the Middle East.

Allison & Busby and Pluto Press, possibly two of the brightest hopes of the period, fared less well though both have now re-emerged with their lists more or less intact. Pluto continues as an independent whilst Allison & Busby was bought by W H Allen, part of the Virgin empire.

A string of new publishers – both specialist and general – also entered the market, rapidly establishing themselves with strong programmes. Bloomsbury, Headline and Sinclair-Stevenson are perhaps the most well-known of these, but other entrants with particularly innovative lists are worth further consideration.

Specialist publishers include Cornerhouse Publications (photography), Element Books (mind, body and spirit), Dedalus Books (fiction), No Exit (crime fiction), Readers' International (fiction in translation) and Third House (gay fiction). All have relatively small lists at present but their prospects look healthy. Niche publishing allows companies to concentrate their marketing efforts on a usually readily identifiable audience and, if they continue to commission and produce the right titles, they should be able to build up a strong market base.

Two other new entrants into the market are Fourth Estate and Serpent's Tail. Their lists are more eclectic though both have a strong base in new fiction. Both, along with Cornerhouse, have been recent winners of the Sunday Times Small Publisher of the Year Award. Serpent's Tail deserve special mention as they have been particularly influential in introducing foreign language authors to the attention of the reading public – no mean feat within an industry that has traditionally treated translated work with extreme caution. Their marketing efforts are also noteworthy. Striking jacket designs have made their titles instantly recognisable and attention to the media has earned them more column inches than many larger competitors – a good example of what can be done by an enterprising publisher with relatively modest resources.

Although UK publishing remains dominated by English presses, publishers such as Mainstream and Polygon in Scotland and Blackstaff in Northern Ireland have made a noticeable impact on the market in recent years. Publishers based in the Republic of Ireland – Brandon and Poolbeg in particular – are also now looking for a bigger share of the British market thus challenging the traditional flow of British books to the Republic.

Voluntary sector, campaigning and community-based publishing with its recent roots in the radical counter-culture of the 1960s and

1970s has also grown visibly. Many, having moved away from publishing the occasional pamphlet, have now established substantive programmes that are the envy of many more commercially based companies.

In the voluntary and campaigning sectors, SHAC and Shelter have lead the way in housing, the Child Poverty Action Group in welfare rights, whilst the Directory of Social Change and Bedford Square Press have developed strong lists covering charities and fundraising. Development, third world and human rights issues have been kept to the fore by the Latin America Bureau, the Minority Rights Group and Oxfam amongst many others. All have become aware of the value of efficient marketing as they compete increasingly with mainstream publishing houses.

Community-based publishing, of the sort pioneered by organisations such as Bristol Broadsides and the Centerprise Publishing Project in London, has perhaps had a rockier ride but still maintains a firm base. Long gone are the slightly shoddy productions that introduced them into the market and the production qualities of material produced by Crocus Books (formerly Commonword) in Manchester and the Yorkshire Arts Circus can stand alongside titles produced by much more commercial houses. Even the Arts Council, which once condemned community publishing as having 'no solid literary merit', are now the administrators of The Raymond Williams Award for Community Publishing.

Booksellers

The decade of the 1980s also saw substantial changes at the retail end of the industry – none more striking than the entry of the Waterstones' chain into the market. Started in 1982, Waterstones has probably done more in recent years to revolutionise the British bookselling scene than any other retailer, large or small. Purchased in 1989 by W H Smith, the company was merged with Sherratt & Hughes to form Britain's largest chain of specialist booksellers.

Waterstones' main strength in capturing market share lay in its ability to show that buying a book could be a pleasurable experience. Large, well-stocked and well-lit stores, open at unconventional hours, attracted customers away from competitors who soon realised that they would have to change to survive.

The Pentos group, Britain's second largest chain, proved the most capable of meeting this challenge and has undergone considerable expansion during the last ten years, culminating in the purchase of Hatchards towards the end of 1990. Like Waterstones', their profile is distinctly upmarket with considerable attention being given to design and presentation.

Pentos has also built a reputation as a leading campaigner against the Net Book Agreement (see Chapter 5) which supports retail price maintenance throughout the UK trade. In general, this campaign is unpopular with the majority of the bookselling and publishing industry and it remains to be seen where it will lead. However, it can probably be assumed that abolition of the NBA would mean the closure or takeover of many smaller shops and chains as the major conglomerates would need to expand their share of the market to compensate for a reduction in margins.

Further details of the smaller chains and a number of independent and specialist outlets may be found in the appropriate sections of this book but it is encouraging to report that, in spite of a number of unhappy closures, much of the invaluable infrastructure provided by the network of 'community' and 'radical' booksellers that emerged in the 1970s and early 1980s remains intact. Although under considerable pressure from the expansion of the major chains in terms both of number of outlets and range of stock, they still continue to provide a valuable alternative to the average high street bookshop.

Liverpool's News from Nowhere, Mushroom in Nottingham, October Books in Southampton, Sheffield's Independent Bookshop and Belfast's Just Books have all become established features of the local culture. Some of the original stalwarts, such as the Fourth of May Bookshop in Edinburgh, have gone. Others have closed but been replaced; Grass Roots Bookshop in Manchester, for example, closed its doors in early 1990 but a new shop – Frontline Books – opened up on the same site at the end of that year.

In London, newer and more specialist shops like Books for a Change and Silver Moon in Charing Cross Road have joined Bookmarks, New Beacon Books, Sisterwrite, Gays the Word, Compendium and many others in providing a service that, in spite of demand, is still not fulfilled by the larger shops and chains.

Distributors and Wholesalers

In many ways the role of a distributor or wholesaler is that of a service industry to the publisher and bookseller, a role that has become increasingly crucial to the success of both in recent years. With a few exceptions, booksellers increasingly carry fewer copies of individual titles and yet the availability of titles in a bookshop is one of the main criteria by which potential purchasers judge their source of supply. As Terry Maher, the Chairman of the Pentos group, stated in *The Bookseller* in early 1990: 'It is service and commitment to the end consumer which must become a number one priority.'

Most large publishers – such as HarperCollins or Random Century – now take the effective distribution of their titles very seriously. They realise that poor distribution results in lost sales and have invested in setting up specialist divisions which can respond to their needs.

Although some of these organisations will consider handling lists other than their own, many publishers are now turning to the growing number of independent specialist distribution companies. They have learned that, in general, these dedicated operations can provide a more efficient and cost-effective service than they can achieve on their own.

Typical of the medium-sized distribution operations are Plymbridge and Biblios. These companies offer a full warehousing, order processing, dispatch and cash-collection service to their clients with charges usually based on a percentage of turnover. However, they are unlikely to consider publishers with an annual turnover of much less than £150,000, who are catered for by a variety of other distributors.

Many of these smaller distribution companies now offer a sales and marketing service in addition to a basic distribution package. This concept has grown in prominence across the whole trade in recent years but, to a large extent, was introduced by the 'alternative' publishing sector in the 1970s with the formation of Third World Publications and Publications Distribution Cooperative. Unhappily, neither of these organisations has survived into the 1990s but they have been replaced by other operations which offer a range of services to a wide spectrum of publishers – both general and specialist. Such companies include Airlift Book Company, Central Books and Turnaround (see Addresses).

Wholesaling too has been a growth area throughout the 1980s with many small and large companies emerging to provide a fast and efficient service to bookshops. Much of their success can perhaps be put down to the failure of many large publishers to distribute their books effectively to an ever growing and competitive network of retail outlets.

2

Planning your Marketing Programme

First Steps

Before planning any marketing strategies for your publications, begin by asking a few fundamental questions. The answers to these will help you decide on your approach to marketing your publishing programme and how best to go about reaching your intended audience:

- What will the book or books you want to publish say?
- Do you have a specific audience you wish to reach?
- Who will be interested enough to want to buy and read it?
- What would be the most effective way of getting the message across to that audience?

If you can't decide on a feasible method of marketing the book, you may have to rethink the form of your communication. You may decide that the material would be better placed in a magazine or periodical which already has established channels of distribution and a regular readership. Or perhaps you should employ another medium such as video or a radio programme to get your message across to its intended audience.

Only once you have considered the points listed above can you start taking editorial and marketing decisions that serve a unified objective. As publishers we are too often guided by aesthetics, vague impressions of costs and mere habits of marketing.

Once you have established who your primary readership is and thought of the possible composition of a wider audience, reduce your readership profile to a realistic spectrum or rank them in order of importance to you. This process of establishing the target readership and other potential readerships will not only allow you to plan your marketing effectively but also will help you to make realistic decisions on how many copies to print, the style of language and various editorial matters from illustrations to indexing. Involve not only those working with you on marketing and promotion but also colleagues with responsibilities for production, design and editing, and even the author(s) of

7

the manuscript. Consider how you will reach the intended audience: for example through bookshops, libraries and direct mail. The format that you choose to publish in may well be determined by the sales potential for each market. Discuss retail and library potential with a trade distributor, repping agency and, if possible, booksellers or librarians.

Allow plenty of time for the editing, production and marketing processes in the run up to publication. Things very often take longer than expected. A commercial publisher will usually allow about six months from receipt of manuscript to finished copies.

Timing

At the back of this book is a publishing check list which provides a step-by-step chronology from initiating the idea to evaluating the effect of your promotion efforts.

Once you have determined the readership you want to reach with your publication you have two primary marketing objectives:

- How to tell them of the publication you want them to read.
- How to get the copies to them.

Your promotion to the public might be with the intention that they buy from bookshops, directly from you by mail order, or a combination of both. If it is your intention that copies should be made available in bookshops, then how do you ensure the bookshop has sufficient copies at the right time to satisfy this anticipated demand?

Orchestrating these two elements is crucial. Poor timing or an incomplete plan will lessen the impact of your publishing and will not do justice to the work of authorship, editing and production.

From the start ensure that one member of the publishing team has at least a coordinating brief for promotion and marketing. They can start collecting addresses and developing ideas from a very early stage. This person should activate the different stages of the marketing plan at the appropriate time during the publishing process.

Schedule your publishing and promotion. Good timing is essential to most promotion campaigns. It may be that your book will tie in well with a forthcoming newsworthy event or anniversary. If so, coinciding publication and achieving media coverage will help sales. On the other hand, publishing on a day when the press will be preoccupied with events such as a Party conference or the publication of a White Paper, will often do little to increase your chances of media coverage.

Aim to have finished copies at least four weeks before the publication date. If you do not have this time in hand, you will lose press coverage and sales that you will never be able to recover. If you are selling to the library supply outlets and through booksellers, ensure that your trade representatives have advance information as far ahead as possible, ideally with copies of the dust wrapper or cover around three months before publication (see Chapter 5 on selling to the book trade). Remember, the more copies of the book that can be sold from advance orders on the day of publication, the easier it will be when it comes to paying the printer.

Identifying Selling Points

Choose two or three selling points for each title that can be used as the basis for the publicity blurb. Express these in lucid and succinct sentences. It is worth remembering:

- It can help if they are dramatic.
- An element of fun or wit may stimulate interest.
- Avoid jargon, tired phrases or complex and abstract language.
- Never use rambling prose; accept that you cannot squeeze in all the vital points your publication makes – you must be selective.

Quite a useful discipline at this stage is to write a blurb of 50–100 words for the outside back cover (or front flap of a dust wrapper). It should identify the topic of the publication and tempt the browser to look inside. Consider emphasising the one most salient point – it may be all that gets across to the customer.

You might consider giving the manuscript to someone well known in the field and asking them to comment on it. The comment, if favourable, can then be used to add weight to your cover blurb.

Ask your author(s) for promotion ideas, useful contacts and a commitment to help with the promotion. You may find it helpful to issue an Author Questionnaire. At the very least this should cover:

- details of full name, address, nationality and a short biographical note;
- a brief statement in the author's own words, on the scope and contents of the book;
- the intended readership.

An example of a comprehensive author's questionnaire is given in Figure 2.1.

Involve your trade representatives or even distributors in planning your promotion, they can often help you avoid disastrous covers or unrealistic print-runs. Even if you think you know it all, they are more closely in touch with the trade and can be invaluable guides. Offer to give a short presentation to your sales reps to ensure they know all that is necessary about the titles and authors.

Figure 2.1 Journeyman Press Author's Questionnaire

Please help us to give your book the best possible publicity and promotion, to reach its target market and to achieve its maximum sales potential. The information you supply here will form the basis of the description of the book on the cover and in catalogues and leaflets aimed at potential buyers. It will also help us to keep our sales staff accurately informed, and ensure that we concentrate on the most appropriate areas of the market. **Please complete and return PART 1 as soon as possible. PART 2 is less urgent but should be returned as soon as it is practical for you to complete it.** Please answer each question as fully as possible, bearing in mind that we sell our books in overseas markets as well as the UK.

We know that filling in this form takes time, but we cannot stress too strongly how important it is that it is fully and promptly completed. Thank you for your help.

PART 1

1. PROVISIONAL TITLE OF BOOK
SUB-TITLE (if any)

PERSONAL DETAILS

2. Full name

Address (Home)   (Work)
Telephone (Home)   (Work)

Which address should we use? HOME/WORK/EITHER
(Please ensure that you inform us of any change of address straight away.)

Your name as it should appear on the book

Your present position

3. Biographical note: please write a short biographical note about yourself (approx 50 words) as you would like it to appear on the book.

Any other previous positions/occupations/activities not covered above

Publications

Citizenship   Date of birth

4. Contributors. If you are the editor of a collected work, please list names, addresses, telephone numbers and affiliations of all contributors.

THE BOOK

5. Why do you believe the book is needed?

6. Describe in about 200 words the subject and structure of your proposed book. This will form the basis for the copy used on the book itself and any promotional material we produce. Please attach a table of contents if possible.

7. Short description: Please also describe your book in about 50 words of consecutive prose, to highlight only the most important points in your longer description.

8. New edition: Is your book a new edition of an already published work? If so, please specify what important new material you have added.

9. Sales features: It is helpful to have some concise 'selling features' that you would highlight for your book. Please list up to six. Please cover topicality, if the book is controversial and if so how and the special qualifications you have for writing it.

Signed
Date

PART 2

THE MARKET

1. What do you see as the book's basic readership?

Does the book have an academic market? YES/NO

If yes, at what level and on which courses?
Please identify the type of institution and the department that would be responsible for the course. Please be as specific as possible for both UK and overseas.

2. Give details of the likely non-academic market for your book:

Industry/Business/Commercial
Trade Union
Professional
Local Government
Other

3. Indicate the size of the market for your book:

(a) UK
(b) USA
(c) Europe
(d) Elsewhere (please specify)

4. List any competing books you know of (detailing author, title, publisher, date and price) and explain why your book should be preferred. Please be as specific as possible:
- How is your book more up to date?
- If your book breaks new ground, how does it do so?
- If the approach is new or different, how is it better?

PROMOTION

5. We aim to promote your book through organisations with which you or your book are connected as well as through appropriate media contacts.

PLEASE ATTACH LISTS OF THE FOLLOWING, **with contact names, addresses and telephone numbers wherever possible**:

- any **associations** or **organisations** whose members might be interested in your book. Please indicate if you would be able to obtain **membership lists** for any of them.
- any bulletins or newsheets of these or other organisations which might carry **promotional inserts** for your book. Please supply full details.
- newspapers, newsletters, bulletins and other journals that may **review** your book. Please make the list as focused as possible.
- any **radio or TV** contacts you have, with name, address and telephone number if possible.
- the names, departments and affiliations of lecturers whom you particularly recommend should receive information about **inspection copies.** We will supply these to academics at our discretion.
- any **key targeted** list of people not covered above. We are always happy to consider sending out a simple flyer to key targeted individuals.

6. Are there any **well-known people** who, because they know you or because of their special interest in the subject of your book, might be asked to give us a favourable **advance opinion** for advertising purposes if they were sent a proof copy? Please give name, address and telephone number.

7. Are there any major forthcoming **conferences** at which your book might be displayed? Please give the name and address of the conference organiser.

8. Is there any **other information** which might help us to sell your book?

9. If journalists wish to contact you shall we give them your number or handle enquiries on your behalf?

10. If invited to do so are you prepared (if necessary without fee) to:

sign copies of your book?	YES/NO
give an interview to the press?	YES/NO
appear on television?	YES/NO
lecture on the subject of your book?	YES/NO

INFORMATION WHICH MAY BE NEEDED TO MEET LEGAL OR FINANCIAL ARRANGEMENTS

11. Do you hold copyright on the work? YES/NO

If not, please state the copyright holder and contact address

What country are you resident in for tax purposes?

Name, address and telephone number of next of kin

Signed
Date

THANK YOU FOR YOUR TIME AND HELP

Costing

The costing of your publishing programme and its resulting profitability will depend to a large extent on the type of publishing with which you are involved. Commercial publishers' main criteria may well be the return on their capital investment, whereas those in the voluntary sector, for example, will have other considerations.

Costing and profitability factors will also be influenced by the type of books you intend to publish. A specialist hardback publisher will be looking to turn a profit on their first printing, while a large school publisher may not expect to see a return until the second or even third printing.

When setting the retail price you will have to consider two primary criteria: first, the production, editing and author costs, which will be determined by negotiations with typesetters, printers and the author, secondly, how much you think the market will bear.

Once these basics are established, you will then need to consider your other overheads. These will include fixed overheads such as rent and staff costs together with variables such as post, publicity, sales and distribution. Part of the income you generate from sales of the book will be allocated to these costs and theoretically anything remaining will constitute your profit.

Let us take as a simple example a first print run for a specialist non-fiction paperback of 3,500 copies put out by a small publisher with a selling price estimated at £8.99.

Example of Costing	£	£
List price		8.99
Less trade discount, average 37.5%	3.37	5.62
Less royalties @ 10% of net	0.56	5.06
Less sales & distribution @ 25% of net	1.41	3.65
Less production costs	1.50	2.15
Less contribution to general overhead @ 25%	1.40	0.75
Less promotion @ 8%	0.45	0.30
Contribution per book		0.30

On a print run of 3,500 copies therefore, assuming 100 copies are distributed gratis (press, author, etc.), this gives a 'profit potential' of £1,020. It will also be interesting to note that a break-even on production, royalty and sales costs will only be reached after sales of 1,438 copies. That is the number of copies you will need to have sold at £5.62 each before you have generated enough income to cover these primary costs. This can be expressed as follows:

$$\frac{3,500 \times £1.50}{£5.62 - (£0.56 + £1.41)} \quad = \quad 1,438 \text{ copies}$$

Of course, there are many different factors involved in the publishing process which will vary extensively from publisher to publisher and from book to book. This example may not be appropriate to your particular circumstance, but it should prove useful as a guide to the necessary considerations.

Pricing your Books

If you are worried that your list price is going to be in excess of the market price, look at the price of new titles from other publishers – the simplest way to do this is to look at advertisements in the half-yearly *Bookseller* – and bear in mind that prices may rise by the time your title is published. If the price is still too high, you will have to look at reducing your overheads in some way or reducing your production costs. *Bear in mind that it is usually very inadvisable to consider printing more copies of a title in order to reduce your unit cost.*

Most books published in Britain are currently net books. That is, under the terms of the Net Book Agreement (see Chapter 5), publishers, or their distributors, sell to bookshops on the condition that the books may not be sold by the bookshops at less than the price determined by the publisher. There are some exceptions to this, such as selling under licence to libraries. School books are generally non-net; that is, they are not covered by the Net Book Agreement and can be sold on by bookshops at whatever price the bookseller determines. Usually, however, books declared non-net are not intended to end up on booksellers' shelves.

Most books require recosting or adjustments made to initial costings before the final retail price is fixed. If you have to quote the price before you have finalised it, make sure you indicate that it is approximate. Although not a hard and fast rule, it is traditional in British publishing (at least since 1971) to price books at amounts ending in 95p although, in line with other products, it has recently become the norm for publishers to price at amounts ending in 99p.

Bookshops earn their money by buying at the retail price less a discount. The discounts given to bookshops vary from 35–45 per cent for trade paperbacks (general, non-specialist titles) to 20 per cent on academic and specialist titles or single-line orders.

Further details of other sales and distribution costs, including an outline of required discounts to booksellers, can be found in Chapter 5 on selling to the book trade.

Design and Format

The general processes involved in designing your books fall outside the scope of this handbook. However, several aspects of design are important for the marketability of a publication.

If you are taking on the design work yourself the general rule is, if you are in any doubt about any major design or production issue, be conventional. That way you run fewer risks. When working with designers give them clear briefs and parameters but don't cramp their creativity by telling them exactly what you would like. You will usually find that they have better ideas.

Bookshops are loath to buy spine-less pamphlets. Apart from getting lost on the bookshelf, pamphlets are of low unit value and do not usually justify the space required for a face out display. If you want to sell through the retail trade you must, if at all possible, bind the publication in such a way that it has a spine on which the title, author's name and your logo can – and should – be printed. In other words, make it into a small paperback.

Avoid A5 dimensions as this will look unprofessional to the bookseller and librarian; it is better to choose a metric demy octavo (216x138mm), perfect bound format (see Glossary). Binding up a few copies in hardback may cost a little more, but can be worthwhile for the library supply market (see the section on selling to libraries in Chapter 7). Some publishers test the market by announcing a hardcover edition as well as a paperback edition well before publication (each edition must have a separate ISBN – see below) and base their final decision on the pre-publication response just before going to press.

Covers and Jackets

Contrary to the old adage, people do often judge books by their covers and the impact of a well designed and informative cover cannot be underestimated. The cover or jacket is one of the most important marketing tools. Essential to bring a book to the attention of the prospective purchaser, it also has a crucial role in advance of publication in the selling process (see Chapters 5, 6 and 7).

If possible use a professional with experience of book cover design. Whatever design you settle on for each title, bear the following in mind:

- Ensure the back cover carries enough information. This should at least include a succinct description of the contents, any advance acclaim or praise, brief author biography, and ISBN/bar code. Finally, include the name of your imprint.

- Use a smaller typesize for the author's name than that used for the title unless he/she is the key selling point.
- Ensure the lettering on the spine reads from top to bottom. It should comprise the title, author(s) and imprint or logo.
- Use strong colours and bold type, but don't over design or fill the front or back with unnecessary clutter.

Extend the shelf life of your publication by avoiding such features as white unvarnished covers that quickly become shop-soiled. If printing the price on the cover remember that, if you are left with copies of the original print run after a year or two, you may well want to increase the retail price to keep abreast of inflation. Placing stickers ('stickering') over the old price as you dispatch copies is not the most interesting aspect of book publishing and your distributors are likely to charge for doing this. If you do use price stickers, have the name of your imprint included on them.

ISBN

The International Standard Book Number scheme (ISBN) was introduced in the 1960s to create a standardised numerical identification system for book publishers. Each edition of every title published should carry a unique ISBN. To obtain an ISBN prefix for your imprint and a list of sequential numbers to allocate to each edition you publish, contact the Standard Book Numbering Agency (see Addresses).

Have the ISBN incorporated in a machine-readable code (bar code) printed on the back cover of the book. This will make it easier for large bookshop chains to log the title onto their computerised stock control systems. Bear in mind the colour used to print the bar code. Some electronic 'wands' that scan bar codes at the point of sale seem unable to decipher codes printed in red, so it is wise to stick to black on a white panel. A full-size bar code looks unsightly so ask for a bar width reduction of 20 microns and truncation of 45% – which is what you see on the back cover of this book. There are many suppliers of bar codes – one tried and tested company used by publishers is Kings Town (see Addresses).

The ISBN should also appear on the copyright page of the book and on all publicity material you produce.

If you are publishing periodicals or books in a series, you may require an International Standard Serial Number (ISSN). (See Publishing in a Series, below.)

Bibliographies

Obtaining entries in bibliographies is one of the cheapest ways of promoting a publication. It usually has a greater impact on library sales than on sales to bookshops, but an entry in *Whitaker's Books in Print* allows booksellers to trace your title when a reader requests it. This is the standard reference tool giving details of all available books in the United Kingdom.

By submitting full details of the ISBN, the title, author, distribution arrangements and bibliographic information on a Whitaker Book Information form at least a month before publication (if you forget, do it after publication) your title will be listed free, first in the subject listing at the back of the weekly *Bookseller* trade magazine and then in *Whitaker's Books in Print*. Either the monthly microfiche edition or the CD ROM Bookbank version is used by most bookshops in the UK. Forms are available from the Book List Editor, J Whitaker and Sons Ltd (see Addresses). Whitaker also publish two special editions of *The Bookseller* in February and August each year. These provide in three sections (publishers' adverts, subject run-down with blurbs and an alphabetical index of titles and authors included) a list of titles that UK publishers intend to bring out over the subsequent six months. Advertising rates and details of how to secure an entry should be requested well in advance from J Whitaker.

The American equivalent of *Whitaker's Books in Print* is *Books in Print* published by R R Bowker and Co (see Addresses). If you have arranged for exclusive distribution through one distributor in the US, send them a note on your letterhead acknowledging them as such and requesting them to apply for listing in BIP for all the titles you wish to sell in the territory. They should then be able to do the rest. Unless it can be classified as poetry, drama, bibliography, art or childrens, each title must have at least 49 pages to be eligible.

Whitaker are also the agents for the British Library Cataloguing in Publication (CIP) programme. To participate in this scheme you will need to provide Whitaker with a completed CIP form for each title at least two months in advance of publication; a typeset entry for inclusion on the copyright page will then be returned. Alternatively a standard wording can be used on the same page of each book you publish indicating that the title has been registered with the British Library. The wording should be as follows: 'A catalogue record for this book is available from the British Library.'

The valuable aspect of CIP is that, prior to publication of each title, the British Library will, free of charge, make an entry in the *British National Bibliography*, on cards through the BNB card service, on magnetic tape as part of the UKMARC exchange tape service and online via the BLAISE-LINE (British Library Automated Information Service). For full details of the service, contact the CIP Development Officer at the British Library National Bibliographic Services or Whitaker (see Addresses).

Information should also be sent to *British Book News*, published by the British Council. This is a monthly survey of new and forthcoming British books and is read by bookbuyers, booksellers and librarians throughout the world. Full details can be obtained from the British Council Publishing Department (see Addresses).

Send details of your forthcoming titles – a dust jacket, cover or advance information sheet will do – and a complete list of your publications to Book Trust (see Addresses). Formally the National Book League, the aims of Book Trust are to promote the role of books in the enrichment of life, to make books and reading more accessible to people of all ages, races and cultures and to protect and further the interest of readers. Part of their service is to provide information to the public and the book trade and they always welcome information on new publications.

Book Trust Scotland (see Addresses) carry out the aims of Book Trust within Scotland, with an emphasis on children's books and Scottish books. Cyngor Llyfrau Cymraeg/Welsh Books Council (see Addresses) promote books with a Welsh interest and books published in Wales through a monthly book list and quarterly magazine *Llais Llyfrau/Book News From Wales*.

The *Radical Bookseller* also includes in each issue a listing of new titles received by the London Labour Library. For inclusion, send one copy of each title to The London Labour Library, c/o Radical Bookseller (see Addresses).

Engaging the services of a bibliographic agency will help booksellers and librarians trace your titles. Book Data is one such company. It covers the UK and overseas, and offers a bibliographic service for publishers by providing details of available titles to booksellers, librarians and institutional buyers. The information is compiled from advance information submitted to Book Data by their client publishers. Full details and rates can be obtained from Book Data (see Addresses). Book Data are also linked into the NERIS information service providing a similar function to the education sector (see the section on promoting your titles to schools in Chapter 7).

In a drive to encourage publishers to improve the accuracy and timing of information about new titles, the Publishers Association have produced a brief guide to the type of information required by the book trade: *Do Your Announcements Tell the Whole Truth About Your Books?* It is available free from the Publishers' Association.

Advance Information

Once you have secured the bibliographical details for your book you will be in a position to prepare an Advance Information (AI) sheet. For most publishers, this will be the initial announcement of a book's

Figure 2.2

ADVANCE INFORMATION FROM
journeyman

NEW BOOK

MARKETING FOR SMALL PUBLISHERS
Bill Godber, Keith Smith and Robert Webb

Marketing for Small Publishers is a step-by-step handbook on the most effective ways to market publications. First published by Inter-Action Trust in 1980, this highly acclaimed book has now been completely revised and updated. It provides a chronological guide from making the initial decision to publish, to deciding on title and format, promoting and selling to the trade, schools, libraries and other specialist markets, and dealing with the media, bookshops and distributors. Essential reading for small publishers, it will also prove of considerable value to marketing departments of large publishers, publications departments within companies and voluntary bodies whose main business is not publishing, and those training to enter publishing.

AUTHOR DETAILS
Bill Godber is Director of Turnaround Distribution. **Keith Smith** is Director of Broadcasting Support Services and formerly publisher at Inter-Action and Export Marketing Manager at William Collins. **Robert Webb** is Publications Marketing Officer at the Minority Rights Group.

SPECIAL FEATURES
- Completely revised edition has been restructured into clearly defined chapters
- Thoroughly researched to incorporate changes in both the 'corporate' and 'independent' sectors of British publishing

READERSHIP
- Small and medium-sized publishers
- The voluntary sector
- Marketing departments of large publishers
- Other organisations that publish books, journals and pamphlets
- Authors
- Training establishments

BIBLIOGRAPHICAL INFORMATION
Publication November 1992   140pp
1 85172 034 0 hardback   £27.50
1 85172 035 9 paperback   £8.99

ORDERS to: Journeyman Press, 345 Archway Road, London N6 5AA
Phone: 081 348 2724   Fax: 081 348 9133

existence and will be produced and circulated some three to six months prior to the anticipated date of publication.

AIs will be mailed to library suppliers and key accounts and used by your representatives and agents (see Chapters 5–7).

AIs are traditionally A4 in size and normally in a portrait format. However, ask your sales representatives if they would prefer horizontal (landscape) versions for convenient presentation alongside the book covers in their folders. Each AI should include the following essential data:

- title and sub-title;
- author(s) or editor;
- publication date;
- price;
- ISBN;
- number of pages and illustrations;
- format and binding(s).

They will also include brief details of the book's subject matter and contents, information on the author(s) and an indication of the intended market and readership. An example of an Advance Information sheet is given in Figure 2.2.

Publishing in a Series

If you plan to publish your titles as part of a series, you may also wish to promote them to the serial and journal market. First obtain an International Standard Serial Number (ISSN) from the UK National Serials Data Centre (at the British Library Bibliographic Services – see Addresses). The number you will be assigned will be for the series title and should appear on each volume, usually on the copyright page. This does not exclude you from also allocating each title an ISBN. Once the ISSN has been allocated, inform the relevant journal and serial bibliographies and request a free entry. The main source of information on regular and irregular series published worldwide is *Ulrich's International Periodicals Directory* (published annually in the United States by R R Bowker – see Addresses). For more details on managing a subscription system see Chapter 7.

Copyright Deposit

On or before publication of each title send a free copy (hardback if available) to the Legal Deposit Office of the British Library (see Addresses). This is a legal requirement and the British Library will eventually send a reminder if you fail to supply a title. Sometime after sending the legal deposit copy to the British Library, you will probably receive a demand under the provisions of the Copyright Act that you send five free copies to a London agent – currently A T Smail (see Addresses) – which will be deposited in: the Bodleian Library, Oxford; the University Library, Cambridge; the National Library of Scotland; the Library of Trinity College, Dublin and the National Library of Wales.

Promoting Your List and Imprint

As soon as your list reaches around six or more titles, publish your own catalogue or publications list. Do not rush the production for careful proofreading is required. Include:

- complete bibliographic details (page numbers, ISBN, etc.);
- a stock list combined with an order form if the list is extensive;
- an indication of which titles are new and the publication dates of forthcoming titles;
- details of where booksellers can order the titles;
- terms of supply.

Standardise the design of your title promotions to give them a recognisable image. This might involve using one design typeface or a consistent style of border around adverts. Use a colophon (publishers' logo) and do not change it – other people will not see it as often as you do.

Request entries, all free, in:

- *The Booksellers Association Directory of Book Publishers and Wholesalers* (Booksellers Association – see Addresses).
- The *Writers' and Artists' Yearbook* (A & C Black, 35 Bedford Row, London WC1R 4JH).
- The *Cassell/Publishers Association Directory of Publishing* (Cassell, Villiers House, 41–47 Strand, London WC2N 5GE. Tel: 071 839 4900).
- *Publishers in the UK and their Addresses* (J Whitaker – see Addresses), the microfiche edition of which is updated monthly.

Two useful directories of small publishers which could also be considered are: the *Small Press Yearbook* published by the Small Press Group and the *Catalogue of Little Press Books* published by the Association of Little Presses (see Addresses).

In the USA, the *Directory of Small Presses* published by Dustbooks (who have also published the *Small Press Review* since 1966), may also be considered. Contact them at Box 100, Paradise, CA 95969. Forms for inclusion in these directories will be sent on request.

The European Book World lists in three volumes and on CD-ROM, publishers, libraries and other book trade addresses throughout Europe. For listing in the publishers section, contact Anderson Rand (see Addresses).

Budgeting for Promotion

Finally, it is important at an early stage in the life of each publication to cost your promotion expenditure into the overall publication budget. Many small publishers in our experience have carefully costed the production expenses of a publication without taking into account the very necessary budget required for promotion.

Although standard formulae do exist, how much money you allocate for publicity will depend to a large extent on the type of publishing in which you are engaged. A campaigning organisation publishing on an important issue, for example, may consider spending more than a small literary publisher. Again, a school text book publisher will want to ensure it can allocate more money for promotion than a general hardback publisher. The other key factor in setting a budget will be the resources available to you around and at the time of publication; even if you think you have a bestseller on your hands, it will not be a great help if you don't have enough money to promote it adequately.

Most commercial, general publishers aim to budget around five per cent of the gross price of each book for promotion purposes and this is probably a good starting point for calculating costs. Obviously, you will need to have this money available before you start to receive any income from sales of your titles so it is important to make sure that you take it into consideration when raising finance.

How you spend your promotion allocation will clearly depend on what you perceive to be the best way of alerting the market to your product. However, the list that follows will give you a few pointers to costs that you should bear in mind:

- Leaflets/catalogues – design and production.
- Leaflet mailings – including list rental, envelopes, stuffing and postage.
- Press advertising – design, typesetting and rates.
- Review copies – unit cost of books plus postage.
- Launch – mailing of invitations, hire of premises, refreshments.
- Display material – posters and point of sale aids.
- Media – unit cost of books, postage and telephone, entertainment.

3

Promotional Mailings and Direct Sales

This chapter looks at ways of reaching your target audience by direct marketing with the aim of promoting or selling books straight to the end purchaser. It covers the essential processes from designing, producing and disseminating direct mail material through to handling and monitoring the response. Direct selling to the public at conferences or other events is also covered. These methods of marketing may prove particularly appropriate for publishers of books aimed at a specialist audience; titles that are unlikely to be widely represented in the average high street store.

Preparing Publicity Material

As well as preparing the blurb for book covers, the skill of copy-writing is useful for writing catalogue entries, Advance Information sheets and other promotional material. It can also be misused. Some principles of copy-writing are:

- Aim to be straightforward and lucid.
- Limit the number of ideas and subordinate clauses carried in one sentence.
- Use the active voice. It is clearer and more vigorous than the passive.
- Express ideas positively. This injunction is better than: Avoid being negative. Never use a double negative.
- Vary the length and form of your sentences to avoid monotony.
- When choosing words prefer the short to the long, the simple to the complex and the concrete to the abstract.
- In your search for clarity be ruthless on redundant words. 'Money is scarce' is better than 'The money supply situation is serious.'
- Vigour is a valuable by-product of brevity. Compare 'This book is best read in the bath' with 'Read this book in the bath.'
- Avoid current horrors such as 'in a large number of cases' for 'many' and 'at this point in time' for 'now'.

- Prose looks less daunting if you keep the paragraphs short. Narrow columns are quicker to read than wide ones.
- Forget that you learned never to use the same word twice. It is sometimes important to do so to be clear.
- Use short prepositions. 'The cost varies with the print-run' is better than 'The cost varies in relation to the print run.'
- Avoid clichés, hackneyed expressions and slogans. They have often run out of meaning.
- Current slang and hip expressions date quickly.

If you have several points to make it can be effective to list and to asterisk them or otherwise single them out.

Never destroy the integrity of your author's work by making false claims. Almost invariably they will backfire on your author and not you.

Designing Publicity

Design publicity material for readability before you design for aesthetics. One colour can be effective. An extra colour (using two different colour printing inks) increases printing costs. Points worth remembering are:

- Keep it simple.
- Reversing out can be effective but ensure your typeface is bold enough to stand out. Sanserif faces are best for this.
- Do not mix several typefaces.
- Use borders or rules to box or separate adverts.
- All artwork should be black on white. Don't use coloured pens.
- If you are in doubt whether something will reproduce, ask your printer's advice.
- Do not crowd. Leaving empty spaces around the copy is effective.
- Use illustrations and symbols if appropriate. Line drawings are safer for production and cheaper than photographs – but don't attempt an illustration yourself unless you are confident your draughting skills are up to it.
- Remember, the publicity material will probably be the first opportunity for people to learn of your publication – it is important to give it a professional appearance.

Distributing Publicity Material

Distributing publicity leaflets and other promotional material is a key ingredient in most publishers' promotion plans. Depending on the type of books on offer, its aim will be to solicit direct cash-with-order sales and/or to alert individuals and institutions to books that can be purchased through the trade.

Methods of distribution include:

- mail-shots;
- inserts in magazines and periodicals;
- via public places such as art galleries and cinemas.

Lists for mail-shots can be compiled either by in-house resources or by rental or purchase. You may also be able to arrange for an organisation to include your leaflet in their mailing. This may be free of charge, but if you have to pay, expect it to be in the region of £50 per thousand. Alternatively, depending on the size of your list, you may decide to offer free copies to the organisation for the staff or the library as payment in lieu.

The normal response rate to a 'cold' mailing to potential purchasers is no more than 2 per cent according to the lore of direct mail in publishing, although of course it varies depending on timing, your address list and the product you are trying to sell. So, if you are paying for a mailing, bear in mind that revenue from 2 per cent of the total mailing should at least pay for the cost of the exercise.

If the leaflet is one you intend to use for several mailings, have a string of letters (A,B,C,D,E, etc.) – also known as a scratch code – included on a clip-off order form when it is typeset. Before printing your leaflets, calculate the quantity required for each separate mailing and instruct the printer to delete the last character from the plate before each quantity is run. This will gradually reduce the length of the code and provide you with separately coded leaflets for each mailing. As you receive orders, you will then be able to identify which of the lists produced a good response.

If promoting through the voluntary sector or campaigning organisations, consider offering the supplier of the list a percentage of the sales made by the mailing rather than paying a fixed fee.

You may wish to reach your target audience by inserting a promotional piece in an appropriate magazine or journal. There may be a weight restriction on inserts, however, and a single sheet flyer could prove better than a folded leaflet. An insert in the right magazine generally produces a better result than advertising (see Chapter 4), but remember that it will probably only be seen by the first person to read the magazine and may even fall out of newstand and library copies before it reaches the reader. Approach likely magazines and ask for their rate card which will include the rate for inserts. You can sometimes negotiate a cheaper rate, especially if you book advertising space as well.

Enclosing promotion leaflets or a publication list in parcels going to mail order customers is worthwhile. However, enclosing a leaflet in bookshop orders is less likely to get to the buyer than if you were to send it directly for their attention.

Most publishers who run mail order services insist that payment is sent with orders. If you don't at least request this, you will be incurring unnecessary expense in issuing pro-forma invoices and chasing up bad debts. It is important to make it as easy as possible for potential customers to make a purchase. The order form should be clear and uncomplicated. Specify the currency you are willing to accept, to whom cheques are payable and include the option of paying by credit card if possible. Don't forget to give your own address on the order form itself and a clear indication if an extra charge is made for postage.

Ensure that you include a rider that will cover you for any possible price increase, especially if you are offering something likely to have a short life at the price stated. An 'allow 7-10 days for delivery', or similar, message will also cut down on phone calls from impatient customers. If you are promoting well before publication, be sure to make this clear by stating the anticipated publication date.

List Brokers

There are several mailing agencies, or list brokers, that specialise in a range of services from providing names and addresses to the physical mailing of publishers' promotion material. Most of them allow you to select the category of recipient your publicity is sent to: libraries, academics with a particular subject interest, named individuals in organisations, etc. Be very specific in your selection or you may be paying for addresses that are completely inappropriate for your needs. You may be able to rent the names and addresses either on a sheet, on labels or on magnetic tape, or you may prefer the agency to arrange the mailing for you. Whatever you choose, you will pay accordingly. You can usually cut your costs if you arrange to share your mailing with pieces from other publishers.

There are many agencies used by publishers. Perhaps the two most well known are IBIS Information Services Ltd and A Mail (see Addresses).

Further information on list brokers and services on offer can be obtained from the British List Brokers Association (see Addresses). The BLBA can give full details of the services provided by those companies that have successfully been elected to membership and who have undertaken to uphold the trading standards recommended in the Association's Code of Practice.

If you decide to do the physical mailing yourself, depending on the amount you are sending out and the destinations, it may be worth consulting the Post Office to find out what discount options are available on bulk dispatches. Generally, this will only be worthwhile if you are sending out 4,000 or more UK-only addresses, all with full postcodes. The Post Office can also supply details of how you can set up reply-paid and 'freepost' arrangements.

Other Ways of Compiling Lists

As an alternative to buying in lists from brokers, you can build up your own from a variety of directories such as the *World of Learning* (Europa) which details academics in universities and higher education establishments throughout the world. Associations and professional bodies may also be prepared to sell you membership lists or allow you access to them. *The Directory of British Associations* (CBD Research) is a good source of contacts.

Building up your own lists can be time consuming and tedious work best done on a computer data-base, but it will provide you with a valuable resource if kept up-to-date.

Register your list with the Data Protection Registrar (see Addresses); this is a legal requirement for all computerised mailing lists.

Another avenue of approach is through booksellers, many of whom run their own specialist mail order service. Booksellers active in your area of interest may well be prepared to include your leaflet in their own mailings. They may make the condition that the order form be overprinted with their name and address.

Mailings to the Overseas Market

If your book has international appeal, explore the possibility of obtaining overseas address lists. This can be achieved either by renting from a list broker in the UK, or from one in your target market.

If your publications carry a particular message, you may be able to find an overseas organisation willing to include your leaflet with their own mailings. Remember that sending thousands of leaflets overseas can work out expensive. If this proves to be the case, explore the cost of having film of the artwork to be sent directly to the organisation concerned for them to coordinate printing; it may work out cheaper.

Handling the Sales

This can sometimes be less straightforward than you may anticipate, particularly if you are handling your own packing and dispatch. Remember that if your publicity is successful you could experience an initial flood of returned order forms. The customers, not unreasonably, will expect to receive prompt delivery of the goods, along with a receipt or invoice.

You will need the right sort of packaging material. A commercial stationery supplier will usually be able to provide a good range of cushioned wrapping, corrugated cardboard and padded bags. A set of scales and current price lists from the Post Office and a franking machine or lots of stamps are essential. It can be time consuming to pack and dispatch lots of parcels so try to anticipate what you will need and when, and enlist help. The Post Office will make parcel collections if you ring your local sorting office in advance.

Do not forget to keep all names and addresses of purchasers – but keep them safe. They are valuable and you will be contravening the Data Protection Act if they fall into the hands of others. Record each sale carefully, together with the date and method of dispatch.

Costing

Before planning any mailings of publicity material, it is important to calculate the costs involved as accurately as possible. This will also be crucial for analysing the results and cost-effectiveness of the exercise. When budgeting a mailing, be sure to allocate money for:

- design of material;
- printing;
- list rental;
- cost of insertion;
- materials (envelopes, labels, etc.);
- postage.

To get a clear idea of the success of your mailing campaign you will probably want to measure response against costs incurred. From an analysis of the response you will be able to calculate the cost per order. This will give you a very accurate idea of the effectiveness of promoting your books in this way.

Book Stalls

Participating in festivals, fairs and other events by having a book stall can be useful for several reasons.

First, you will (hopefully) be selling publications directly to your customers without incurring any postage costs or having to give a book trade discount.

Secondly, it is an ideal opportunity to meet the people who buy and are interested in what you publish. Discussing your books with potential or actual buyers can help you take a more objective look at the books you know so well. Teachers, librarians and readers may complain or compliment, make valuable suggestions on the form or content of your list, or even give you ideas on new areas of promotion. It is also an ideal opportunity to see and be seen. Other stall holders will be just as interested as you are to see what else is new and available in the field. When participating in selling fairs, the following points are worth remembering:

- Take along a cash float with sufficient change and plenty of catalogues and publicity leaflets.
- Make sure that your display looks professional and promotes the image you want.
- Meeting other publishers may result in planning a mutually beneficial promotion, or simply in an exchange of opinions and ideas.
- Have an informed, lively attendant who can respond to questions but who is prepared to stop persistent chatterers from blocking the stall.

Think carefully, however, about the costs in ratio to how much you could hope to sell. Although you will ideally be selling throughout the duration of the event, the cost of renting stalls can vary enormously and the expense of producing special promotional material, travelling and staffing could be prohibitive. Try to find out beforehand:

- how many people are expected to visit;
- where you will be located (ideally near the tea and coffee area);
- where the organisers are advertising the event;
- about security overnight if the event lasts for more than a day.

Sharing a stand or taking one or two other publishers' catalogues or titles to display for a charge are ways of keeping the costs down.

Occasionally the bookselling aspect of an event is organised by a local bookshop with the input of invited publishers who will staff the stalls and then invoice the bookshop for stock sold, less the usual discount.

4

The Media

Ensuring media coverage for your publications will be an important part of a successful marketing plan. This can be achieved through reviews, features, news coverage and advertising.

Although you may find dealing with editors and journalists time consuming and often frustrating, a successful media campaign can sell books; furthermore it will enhance your profile with the general public and with the trade.

Review Coverage

Few products are so widely exposed by the mass media in such an organised manner as books. Bear this in mind in your planning and remember that a review or mention in a newspaper or magazine is about the best free advertising you could hope for.

Compile your review list – the names and addresses of those people to whom you are going to send review copies – from authors' contacts, your contacts and periodical directories (see the end of this chapter for a list). Try to direct material to a named individual at each newspaper and magazine on your list. If you don't have a name to hand, ring to ask either who the review or literary editor is, or whether there is someone with a particular interest in the subject you have published on. Do not rely on well wishers suggesting names unless you can be sure of their sources. Sending a book for review addressed to a journalist who left a magazine some years ago is unprofessional and could well prove to be a waste of time. If your book ends up on the wrong desk or is simply addressed to 'The Editor', there is always the chance that the right person will never get to see it.

It may help to ring the reviewer or editor after a week to see if she or he received the book, whether they have had the time to look at it and if there is any likelihood of coverage. Do not be pushy but do briefly mention any publicity you have planned or any other points that may persuade the reviewer that your title is of interest. Do not plague reviewers though, or you will lose out in the end.

Occasional and sympathetic freelance reviewers can be asked to contact their editors to see if they will accept a review, but think hard before asking personal friends of the author to review the title. It can turn out to be distressing.

It is sometimes claimed that even bad reviews can sell books. Readers forget the damaging remarks but remember the title or author.

Enclose a review slip (an example is given in Figure 4.1) in each copy detailing the title, author, price and publication date and requesting a copy of any review together with your name as the contact person for further information. State that no review should appear before publication.

Figure 4.1 Review Slip

Bloggs Books
1 High Street, Anytown, AN3 3BB

Please find enclosed a review copy of:

Title:	Cooking with Heat
Author:	Ivor Napron
Publication Date:	Thursday 1 April 1995
Price and Format:	£5.99 paperback, 226 pages

Please ensure no review appears before publication date. Notification of any coverage would be appreciated. For further information contact Pat Bloggs on 123 456 7890.

You may want to increase this to a longer review note that gives a brief resume of the publication with notes about the author and the details you would want to appear with each review. It can be frustrating to see a title which you are selling predominantly by mail order reviewed without giving an address for obtaining it or a note of how much money to send.

When planning the dispatch of review copies, it is important that sufficient lead time is allowed to ensure that reviews coincide with the book's publication date. Literary editors of daily and weekly publications will expect to receive review copies some four to six weeks before publication. Monthly magazines often require considerably longer and it may well be worth approaching key periodicals with proof copies – the sense of preview can raise interest.

Finally, it is worth noting that there are a few periodicals that will feature on most review lists for non-specialist titles. These are read by many people in the book world, as well as a large number of book buyers: *British Book News, Literary Review, London Review of Books, The Sunday Times,* and *The Times Literary Supplement.*

News and Feature Coverage

An alternative way of obtaining press coverage is in the form of a news item or feature article rather than a review.

Develop a news angle if you have a newsworthy topic. You can link into a relevant event around publication day or pick up on a current topic of concern by unveiling a new fact, figure, slant or remedy. There is some truth in the cliché that the press are drawn to human interest stories and forebodings of doom. An organisation concerned with the environment may launch a new publication or report by announcing a new figure or statistic, for example, that three in five of Britain's bathing beaches do not meet European standards.

If you have not got interesting news material, don't waste time approaching news desks, concentrate instead on obtaining feature coverage. This will not always be easy for the small publisher but do persevere and, if you think it will help, encourage your authors to write press articles on the topic of the publication. Suggest to targeted feature editors that an interview with your author would make interesting copy.

Press Releases

If you are announcing your book as a news story, or are trying for feature coverage, emphasise the salient points in a press release.

- Restrict releases to no more than two one-sided A4 pages.
- Always use double-spacing.
- Be brief and make the main arresting points in the first paragraph.
- Some journalists will quote verbatim from a press release; word them with this in mind.
- If giving direct speech for them to lift, be sure to put it in quotation marks and identify the speaker.
- Beware of trying to write a racy story.
- State whether the author is available for interview.
- Always give your name and phone number (both day and evening).
- Highlight the price, page numbers, binding, publication date and ISBN in the release.

It is also advisable to specify an embargo on the release. An embargo is a convention which requires the press not to publish the material until the stated time and day – normally on publication day or the day before publication. Embargoes help to reassure journalists that no other papers are likely to run the story before their own. You may, however, consider setting a separate embargo date a few days earlier for radio and TV. The press does draw on radio – in particular local – for news stories.

As with all media contact, ensure that releases are directed to named individuals wherever possible. About 90 per cent of press releases do not lead to coverage, usually because they are not judged newsworthy, are squeezed out or because the release is too long or badly presented. Use the telephone selectively to follow up a release but be brief and to the point, and avoid phoning shortly before press time when journalists may be too busy to deal with telephone calls. Convey your enthusiasm but be realistic. Do not forget to send your press releases to the domestic and overseas news agencies, the main ones being the Press Association and Reuters (see Addresses) who send out stories about events to subscribers. For a charge of around £200 per 300 words, Two-Ten Communications (see Addresses) will disseminate press releases on-line to newsrooms throughout England, Wales and Scotland.

Some syndication agencies are now beginning to offer video press releases. If used sensibly, they can provide imaginative ways (albeit expensive) of getting your message across that are not possible with more traditional methods.

Targeting the Local Media

A survey conducted by the Independent Broadcasting Research Unit in 1988 showed that 21 per cent of people looked to local radio for local news and 58 per cent looked to the local newspaper (36 per cent bought, 22 per cent free). With this in mind, contact your author's local papers and radio stations and make it clear that you have a local author. It is sometimes worth contacting the central offices of the local newspaper chains who might circulate a story to their papers.

Research carried out by the Media Project at the Volunteer Centre has shown that radio is unsurpassed in its intimacy of approach with difficult subjects. If your book concerns a personal story or an issue such as drug dependency or homelessness, give local radio priority in your media campaign.

Local and community radio stations are always looking for suitable material. It is relatively easy to obtain coverage, although it is sometimes difficult to measure its effectiveness. If you can arrange for an author to be interviewed by the BBC Local Radio Programme Services Unit (see Addresses), they will syndicate it to the growing number of BBC local radio stations around the country.

It is possible to obtain syndication to most of the independent local radio stations and community stations (a list is available from the IBA) through syndication agencies. For the cost of a few hundred pounds, an agency will record a tape which it then offers to local radio stations for transmission. There is no guarantee that the stations will take the tape. If you get a piece on Independent Radio News (see Addresses), however, it will automatically be broadcast on many local commercial stations. Many of the large hospital radio stations (currently around 35) also use syndicated news tapes.

If your story is not strong enough for syndication, you or your regional contacts will have to work at local angles and contact the stations direct. A list of producers is available from most radio stations and material should be sent at least a fortnight in advance. Many stations also have open days and it may be worth you or a regional contact joining the list of visitors to get an idea of how local radio operates.

Do not forget the regional offices of BBC Television, some of which produce their own local news magazines, or the regional commercial TV stations.

Radio and Television

If you think your title can pick up feature coverage on national television and radio, choose specific programmes and send the producer, researcher or programme planner a personalised letter together with a press release giving full information on how to obtain a review copy and details of when the author is available for interview. Follow up on the phone to make sure they have received your news release and tell them if there has been any take up by other stations. *The Blue Book of British Broadcasting* has a comprehensive listing of broadcast channels and stations and is available from Tellex Monitors Ltd (see Addresses). The *BFI Film and TV Handbook* is a useful source of press contacts and addresses of cable and satellite television channels.

As with the opportunities offered by more radio wavelengths, the changes in European television in the 1990s and beyond may well open up new possibilities both for the voluntary and the commercial sector. Cable television, satellite television, over-the-air local TV, an increase in regional TV and an enhanced teletext capable of carrying ordinary typefaces and photographs could eventually provide imaginative new media for publicising books.

Do not forget the BBC World Service's regular news and feature programmes. For a full list of programmes, contact their headquarters (see Addresses).

Remember also that Voice of America has a London office (see Addresses) and may be willing to interview your author if the book is of sufficient interest.

Interviewing

If you send authors to broadcast it is your responsibility to ensure they know what to expect. Give them details of:

- the name of the contact person;
- the time of the interview;
- where to go and how to get there;
- the name and nature of the programme;
- the length of interview and whether it is live or recorded.

Depending on your author's experience of the media, it may be a good idea to accompany them to the studio.

Make sure the programme has received a copy of the book at least two days beforehand and is well briefed on its content. It is also your job to ensure that your author can provide a succinct and engaging interview. In all cases ensure that your title receives a plug or at least a full mention at the start or the end of the interview. Brief your author to remind the presenter and producer – and have a note written down – of what you would like them to say when topping and tailing the interview.

If the book has arisen from a campaign, ask the author to give the phone number where people can follow up the subject under discussion and be sure to tell the producer and the receptionist at the radio or TV station where people can get in touch with you. If applicable, brief appropriate office staff on what was said during the interview and tell them how to handle follow-up calls.

Be supportive of your authors. They may appear to be basking in all the glamour of broadcasting but they are in the hot seat and it is mainly their handiwork which is being held up for public examination. A phone call to them after hearing the interview can be a rare tonic. Do not despise a phone call or postcard of thanks to the programme.

The fact that a reporter files or records a story doesn't automatically mean that it will appear. The editor may cut it out.

Be prepared for misreporting. Seek redress but don't invest a lot of time or emotional energy unless you think the real gain is going to be valuable.

Book Launches

A launch is an occasion or event just prior to publication. It can serve a number of purposes:

- to draw media attention to a new book;
- to thank those involved in its publication;
- to encourage trade support.

Consider a party, a talk, an event such as a reading or a press conference. Whichever you choose will need careful planning; there is nothing more embarrassing than a launch attended only by yourself and your author!

Launches can be expensive and you should consider carefully whether there are benefits to be gained from holding one. These days most publishers will only consider them for important lead titles. A press conference should only be held if you have a genuine newsworthy item.

If you decide to go ahead, whatever you arrange must be tightly organised. Lunch time or early evening is a good time for the press; mid-week is generally preferable to Monday or Friday. Location is also important; don't expect the press to travel far.

You will need to make sure someone is available to coordinate activities and ensure that everything runs smoothly. If a discussion is part of the launch, you will need someone to chair it and make sure all relevant points are covered. A prominent personality with an interest in the subject covered by the book will help to draw in the crowds.

The invitation should be brief and to the point but can be accompanied by a press release. Remember to give the date, time, venue and details of any guest speakers. Consider including a map of how to get there if appropriate. Give your telephone number for RSVPs and the name of someone at your end prepared to take the calls. They should also be responsible for checking off who has accepted and who actually turns up.

Send the invitations out a couple of weeks before the event. Your author should be able to help you draw up a list of press and media contacts and may also want to invite friends, family or colleagues.

There may also be photo opportunities. Do not rely on the press to send along their own photographers. Hire your own if you think it worthwhile.

Make sure there is a sufficient stock of books on display and that someone is responsible for taking money if you are selling copies.

A few days before the event, try to get an idea of how many people you expect to attend and arrange for an adequate supply of food and drink.

Finally, ensure that all your costs are kept within a planned budget.

Monitoring the Results

Checking up on the media coverage you have achieved can be a tiresome and expensive business. Although you will have requested copies of reviews, there is of course no guarantee that these will all materialise. The cheap (but time consuming) option is to check out as many periodicals as possible in your local library or friendly newsagent or simply to buy those you think are most likely to cover your book. Complement this by phoning those not widely available.

If you are confident of wide media coverage, a much more expensive but obviously more effective option is to engage the services of a press cutting agency who will monitor the media for mentions of your book or imprint. Some of these are listed in the *Writers' and Artists' Yearbook*. Find out what media they cover and how much they charge; be prepared for it to be expensive.

Remember to tell your booktrade sales representatives what publicity you expect as soon as you can. Booksellers are not always impressed with promises of media coverage, but if the publicity has a local angle or is obviously going to generate some interest amongst customers then the bookseller is far more likely to order confidently. Send the reps copies of any press coverage immediately it appears.

Do not misplace the press cuttings – the quotes, if favourable, will come in handy for the back cover of any reprints or subsequent editions.

Press Advertising

Many publishers are sceptical of the usefulness of advertising. It pleases most authors and may encourage review editors to cover your titles – but does it sell books? Certainly review or feature coverage is cheaper and more credible than advertising.

If you do decide to advertise, choose your paper or journal carefully and design your advert with the readership in mind. *British Rate and Data*, updated monthly, gives circulation figures and advertising rates for most newspapers and periodicals. BRAD also provides rates for advertising on TV and radio, on buses, tube stations and in other public places; such media will be beyond the reach of most marketing budgets but can provide some imaginative ideas for the ambitious small publisher. Details can be obtained from BRAD (see Addresses).

You can sometimes negotiate discounts when advertising trade is slack. If a magazine rings you, they are generally short of advertisers to fill space in the next issue and will be open to negotiation. Special publishers' rates are also available in some newspapers and magazines.

Write advertising copy addressed to the reader, not from the publishers, for example 'A book that tells you ...' rather than 'We have published a book ...' It is not what you say but the way it is heard.

Getting people to read the title of the publication or merely making them aware of its existence is often as useful as saying something substantial about the publication. In other words, use brief copy but always mention the title.

Place advertisements after reviews of a title rather than before.

Evaluating Advertising

Evaluating the response from advertising is easiest when you are inviting readers to order by post. By including a department number in the address, you will then be able to monitor each response as the orders come in. You may also find giving a telephone number for credit card sales will help improve the take up. Remember, however, many readers may purchase through a bookshop and the benefits of advertising are thus almost impossible to gauge accurately.

Ultimately, adverts may be more useful in reminding readers of the existence of an imprint than in selling specific books; accordingly, directing promotion of your imprint to the trade may prove more beneficial than promoting a particular title. The exceptions here are of course the promotion of specialist titles in periodicals with very specific readerships.

Media Directories

Other useful aids in building up press lists and review lists are directories.

Willings Press Guide (British Media Publications, Windsor Court, East Grinstead House, East Grinstead, West Sussex, RH19 1XE. Tel: 0342 326972). This gives the names of virtually all national and local newspapers and periodicals in the UK.

Writers' & Artists' Yearbook (A & C Black, 35 Bedford Row, London WC1R 4JH. Tel: 071 242 0946). Published annually for over 80 years this directory details UK, Irish and Commonwealth newspapers and periodicals as well as a wealth of other information.

Benn's Media Directory (PO Box 20, Sovereign Way, Tonbridge, TN9 1RQ. Tel: 0732 362666). Available in a UK and an international edition. Both volumes, published annually, give details of key personnel, circulation figures, readership, advertisement rates, etc. for newspapers, magazines and periodicals, as well as giving comprehensive information on TV and radio stations, publishing houses, media agencies and other groups and organisations. Current prices are around £90 each volume.

PNA Media Guide (PNA Services Ltd, Communications House, 210 Old Street, London EC1V 9UN. Tel: 071 490 8111). PNA is a media information and press release distribution company serving the public relations industry. The Guide, listing all UK editorial media including newspapers, trade journals, radio and TV stations, is published in six issues per annum. The cost for all six is currently £190.

PIMS Media Directory (PIMS Ltd, Faber Court, 4 St John's Place, St John's Square, London EC1M 4AH. Tel: 071 250 0870) is published monthly, listing names of editors, correspondents and freelancers working for the press, television and radio. The cost is currently £240 for twelve issues.

Ulrich's International Periodicals Directory (available in the UK from Bowker-Saur Ltd., Borough Green, Sevenoaks, Kent TN15 8PH. Tel: 0732 884567).

Charities and Broadcasting (The Directory of Social Change, 169 Queens Crescent, London NW5 4DS. Tel: 071 284 4364) contains some useful advice for the voluntary sector on securing coverage on radio and TV.

5

Selling Through the Book Trade

Most publishers, regardless of size, sell the majority of their titles through bookshops and other trade outlets. Although for some specialist publishers the book trade may be of only marginal relevance, anyone seriously engaged in book publishing will undoubtedly benefit from a basic understanding of trade practice and an awareness of the trade's main components.

The Net Book Agreement

Before you start selling your titles into the trade, it is important to have a rudimentary understanding of the Net Book Agreement (NBA).

Dating from the turn of the century, the NBA is a legal agreement between publishers and booksellers centring around the implementation of retail price maintenance in the UK book trade. It affects the vast majority of titles published in the UK which are classified as 'net books' and which may not be sold to the public at a lower price than that fixed by the publisher. Certain books – most commonly school texts – are classified as 'non-net' and, although they usually carry a recommended price, fall outside the scope of the agreement and may be sold at whatever price deemed suitable by booksellers.

There are exceptions to the agreement which cover the sale of 'net books' into libraries, schools and certain other institutions and those wanting further information should contact the Publishers Association.

In general, the NBA is viewed by publishers and booksellers alike to be beneficial to the trade and to the book buyer. It encourages bookshops to stock a large and diverse range of titles safe in the knowledge that their customers would not be able to purchase a particular title at a cheaper price elsewhere. Such wide stockholding in turn supports the publishing industry by enabling publishers to produce titles unlikely to achieve bestselling status. Finally, but perhaps the main thrust of the agreement, is that the public benefits from the diverse choice of publications available.

Since the late 1980s, however, these views have been strongly challenged with the Pentos group (the country's second largest chain) certainly being the most vociferous opponent of the agreement. They argue that the NBA is an anachronism not appropriate to today's retailing climate and should be abolished, that booksellers, like other retailers, should be allowed to discount their goods and compete on the basis of price and that this would lead to increased book sales, not less, and greater consumer choice.

Supporters of the agreement, including the Publishers Association, the Booksellers Association and the majority of publishers and book-sellers, maintain that abolition would lead to the destruction of the trade as we know it today. Small independent shops would be forced to close, unable to compete with the major chains in a price-cutting war, book prices would be artificially pumped up to allow for greater discounts and choice would be reduced as shops concentrated their energies on bestsellers.

It remains to be seen which of these two positions will prevail but, dangerous as it may be to speculate, it seems likely that, despite heavy attacks currently being made, the NBA will be with us for some years to come. Initial experiments by the chains in price-cutting appear to have had little effect on overall book sales and a price cutting war between the major chains resulting in reduced margins would be unlikely to benefit anyone.

As a publisher, it will be up to you to decide whether to price your books as net or non-net.

Bookshops

Perhaps not surprisingly, bookshops are by far the largest outlets for British publishers. Current estimates suggest that over 60 per cent of publishers' sales are made through bookshops and other retail outlets.

For pamphlets, the proportion of bookshop sales will be much smaller and in all but rare cases will be surpassed by mail order sales.

It has often been said that the distribution of bookshops within the UK is uneven, with a high concentration in middle-class areas. To an extent this is still true but the recent expansion of the high street chains, the development of the community bookselling network and a wider variety of retail outlets selling books has gone some way to counteract this situation. However, although this has meant that books are perhaps more accessible to a greater number of people than ever before, whether or not the range of publications available has widened significantly remains questionable. The Arts Council report *Literature Belongs to Everyone* covers the whole area of access to literature in detail.

Throughout the 1980s the number of retail outlets selling books increased dramatically and it is currently estimated that some 60,000 retailers (Euromonitor) now carry books in some form or another. Much of this increase came from the growth of non-specialist retail outlets now selling books, a trend that is likely to continue into the next decade and one that will be accelerated should the Net Book Agreement be abolished.

At present, however, the 7,500 or so specialist booksellers (including branches of the major chains) still have a firm hold on the retail book market, accounting for some 60 per cent of total sales in 1990.

Table 5.1 illustrates the breakdown of sales over one year by type of outlet.

Table 5.1: Sales of Books by Type of Retailer 1990

	£m
Booksellers	955
Mixed retail	400
Confectioners, tobacconists and newsagents (CTNs)	80
Newsagents/stationers	35
Food retailers	20
Other retailers	40
Carry in	60
Total	1,590

Source *Euromonitor*

Selling to Bookshops

As a publisher, bookshops are major partners in your marketing activities and anyone interested in the sales and promotion side of publishing should familiarise themselves with as many of them as is possible.

Details of most of the booksellers in the UK can be gleaned from the *Booksellers' Association Members Directory* but a consideration of some of the major companies is worthwhile.

Major Retail Outlets

British retail bookselling is dominated by a handful of large chains and independently run stores and whatever type of books you are selling, it is almost certain that you will need to deal with these major outlets. Here is a selection of the larger companies, their discount requirements and current buying practices.

W H Smith Henry Walton and his wife Anna opened a small news-stand in Little Grosvenor Street, London in 1792. Their grandson William Henry Smith saw the opportunities offered by books and the new railway system. In 1848 he started signing contracts for sole bookstall rights on the various lines. It is reported that:

... the rapidly increasing travelling public were delighted to find these new W H Smith bookstalls provided not only newspapers, but books, candles to read them by and even rugs to keep the readers warm.

By 1990, their retail chain in the UK operated from 480 shops (including station bookstalls and airports) plus outlets in Brussels, Paris and Amsterdam. Since these account on different estimates for between 12 and 20 per cent of the UK book market and have somewhat different procedures from other shops, they require looking at in some detail.

At the time of writing, only the 50 biggest branches in the chain see reps, and even then only for major publishers. It is likely, though, that in the near future they will not be seeing reps in their stores at all, except for a small number of branches which have expanded ranges in certain classifications (e.g. Birmingham and Reading for Science Fiction and Fantasy, Oxford and Cardiff for Maps and Guides). The reason given for this is that new point of sale technology gives the group more confidence to buy for the whole chain centrally from their head office in Swindon. The only exception to this is in the case of books of specifically local interest, where reps may still contact the relevant branch directly.

When approaching Smith's, your first task will be to make contact with the appropriate buyer or product manager. There are currently seven of them, all based in Swindon. Between them they cover the following areas: Younger Children (0–7), Older Children (8+), Current Hardbacks, Paperback Fiction, Reference & Technical, Leisure & Travel and Bargain & Promotional Books. If in doubt, you can call Swindon to ascertain into which category your books fall.

Product Managers at Swindon will normally want to make their buying decision on sight of a finished copy about six weeks prior to the publication date. You must bear this in mind if your titles are likely to have a wide appeal to the WHS market. It may well mean that you will have to hold stock for six weeks after printing before you can start invoicing. This may not be too much of a problem for the large publisher, but it could play havoc with your cash flow if your resources are stretched.

You can deal with the buyers by letter and phone but a visit to Swindon to meet them face to face is recommended and is more likely to produce results. They will be keen to know what plans you have for publicity and, if they accept your title for sale in their outlets, will want to know that you can arrange delivery to Swindon at least 12 working days prior to publication to enable distribution to their branches to be completed by the publication date.

If you are a small publisher, you may well find W H Smith's terms fairly steep. They probably average 47 per cent discount on non-technical hardbacks and 50 per cent discount on paperbacks (Price Commission). You are unlikely ever to get them below 45 per cent if they are buying for central stocking at Swindon or for a 'scale out' to their main branches.

Your books will normally be taken on a returnable basis and if your title does not sell, they will insist on the right to return. Be aware that the returns may not be in 'mint' condition and be careful of over hyping your books and ending up with a warehouse full of unsaleable copies.

Publishers have many different views of the WHS chain but being a relatively small publisher need not be a negative factor when approaching them as long as you can absorb their terms of trading. A lot of their current suppliers are small publishers who operate in specialist niches (business, religion, pets, photography etc). They are less likely, however, to be receptive to one-off publishing ventures. Although the reception you receive is usually reasonable, over 40,000 books are submitted to them every year and they will not be slow to reject your titles if they do not feel them suitable for their needs.

The Retail Marketing Division is at Greenbridge Road, Swindon, Wilts SN3 3LD. Tel: 0793 616161.

John Menzies John Menzies PLC has grown from a small select bookshop opened by John Menzies in Princes Street, Edinburgh, in 1833. It was unusual in having a wholesale department for the trade which proved most successful.

Like W H Smith, Mr Menzies saw the opportunities offered by railway bookstalls and by 1858 had contracts for the lease of bookstalls in many stations throughout Scotland.

Since then Menzies has grown considerably, expanding into England and Wales. They control over 200 shops and over 60 bookstalls of which approximately 100 shops have book departments graded A to D. Although generally considered to be the W H Smith of Scotland, over half of these branches are south of the border. In 1987, they bought the Hammicks retail chain and wholesale business, thus expanding further into the British book trade.

John Menzies purchasing decisions for new titles and basic stock selection are controlled centrally and, like many large chains, monitored by a sophisticated EPoS (Electronic Point of Sale) system. This system is linked in to automatic ordering and delivery through the wholesale division of Hammicks. To sell into the Menzies chain, you will need to contact the Book Merchandise Department at their Edinburgh office. Terms of supply are likely to be similar to those of W H Smith. If a decision is made to purchase on a national basis, a scale-out order will be raised through Hammicks and delivery instructions will follow.

Repeat orders for scaled-out titles or special customer orders for books are placed by individual shops. For titles of local interest, authority can be given to sell into appropriate shops on a direct basis.

Contact the Book Merchandise Department, Hannover Buildings, Rose Street, Edinburgh EH2 2YQ. Tel: 031 225 8555.

Blackwell Retail Blackwell Retail is a division of B H Blackwell Ltd which also controls the two Blackwell publishing companies and JMLS, the Nottingham based library suppliers.

Its largest retail branch is the Blackwell shop in Oxford but the group controls some 55 other branches trading under a variety of different names. These include the Georges chain in Bristol, Bissets in Aberdeen, Lears in Cardiff and several outlets in Reading. Each shop supplies a wide range of general books, although many branches additionally have a strong line in academic titles.

Each shop in the chain purchases independently and can be visited by reps. Their head office is at Hythe Bridge Street, Oxford OX1 2ET. Tel: 0865 792792.

Books Etc This London based company opened its first shop in 1981 and by 1990 had nine outlets in Central London. Further expansion is planned.

Each shop purchases independently and may be visited by representatives. They are extremely unlikely to stock any publisher's titles offered at a less than 40 per cent discount and may require more. Accounting is handled centrally at 118–20 Charing Cross Road, London WC2. Tel: 071 379 6838.

Foyles Perhaps one of the most famous bookshops in the world, Foyles has a mixed reputation amongst publishers and bookbuyers. However, the sprawling shop in London's Charing Cross Road generates sales in excess of £10 million per annum and therefore should not be ignored by the budding small publisher.

Reps may visit all departments in the store but note that orders taken must be approved by the general manager prior to supply. Accounting is handled at 119–25 Charing Cross Road, WC2. Tel: 071 437 5660.

Hammicks Formed in 1968 but sold to John Menzies in 1987, Hammicks has some 30 branches including a specialist legal bookshop in Fleet Street, London.

Reps may visit the shops in the chain and can sell into their wholesale division which supplies their own shops as well as branches of John Menzies and the wider book trade. Accounting is handled centrally by the head office at Unit 18–20, Rosevale Road, Parkhouse Industrial Estate, Newcastle-under-Lyme, Staffs ST5 7QT. Tel: 0782 561000.

Heffers William Heffer started bookselling in Cambridge in 1876 and the company now runs five bookshops in the city: a paperback shop, a children's bookshop, a general shop and an antiquarian bookshop in addition to the main branch in Trinity Street. Retail sales account for over 50 per cent of the group's turnover, with remaining sales coming from their extensive mail order operation, library supply and a children's book club.

Reps may visit all retail outlets which buy independently. Accounting is handled at Rustat House, 60 Clifton Road, Cambridge DB1 4FY. Tel: 0223 358351.

Pentos Pentos is the second largest chain of specialist retail booksellers with a turnover of £85 million in 1990. With a claim of 10–11 per cent of the UK retail book market, they are a considerable force in British bookselling.

The company entered bookselling in 1972 when it purchased the Hudsons chain in the Midlands and expanded further with the purchase of Dillons in London in 1977 which is now generally considered the group's flagship. In addition to 50 or so shops trading under the Dillons banner, the group also controls 13 Athena Bookshops and all branches of Hatchards and Claude Gill, which it purchased in 1990. The Hodges Figgis shop in Dublin is also owned by Pentos, as is The Economist Bookshop in London.

All shops in the Pentos group can be repped individually. Accounting is handled centrally through Pentos Retailing at Berwick House, 35 Livery Street, Birmingham B3 2PB. Tel: 021 236 6886.

John Smith & Son Founded in 1751, John Smith has its main branch in Glasgow's St Vincent Street and eight other outlets in towns and universities throughout Scotland. In addition to their retail branches, the company also runs a thriving library supply operation concentrating on the academic market.

Reps may visit all shops. Terms of supply are negotiable, but expect to give 40 per cent discount on general titles. Accounts are handled at 69 Kent Road, Glasgow G3 7LG. Tel: 041 221 7472.

Waterstones/Sherratt & Hughes Waterstones opened their first branch in 1982 and since then have arguably done more to change the face of high street bookselling than any of the other multiples. All outlets are based in prime locations and with their distinctive livery have an up-market feel to them. Late night and Sunday opening are regular features.

In 1989, 50.5 per cent of the company was sold to W H Smith and merged with Smith's specialist bookselling chain, Sherratt & Hughes. This new company, Waterstone Investments, incorporates some 90 outlets making it the largest chain of specialist booksellers in the UK. The group also has branches in Dublin, Cork and Amsterdam and is expanding into the US market with stores in Boston and other major cities.

Each shop buys independently and may be visited by reps. Head office is at Ixworth House, 37 Ixworth Place, London SW7. Tel: 071 584 4448. Accounting is handled centrally at the W H Smith headquarters in Swindon.

Repping to Bookshops

The most effective way to persuade a bookseller to order stock of your titles is to arrange for a visit by a sales representative. Regular calls to bookshops will build up an awareness of your titles to a degree that mounds of leaflets and catalogues never will.

Although repping is invaluable, it is also time consuming and expensive and many small publishers contract out their repping (see Chapter 6). Whether you contract out your repping or do it yourself, you will need to know what is involved. Only by having a clear understanding of how representatives operate can you assess the success of your own or your agent's efforts.

Before beginning a repping trip, telephone to make appointments with the appropriate buyers in each shop. If for any reason you are unable to keep your appointment, make sure you call as soon as possible to rearrange it. Aside from simple courtesy, this is an essential part of the etiquette of repping.

More than anything else, for each title you must know:

- what it is about;
- why it is being published;
- to whom it is addressed;
- what publicity it is likely to receive;
- what the competition is;
- who the author is;
- what terms you can offer;
- what the ISBN and price are.

In addition, you should know what the bookshop you are visiting sees as its main market. It also reassures booksellers to know that the orders they place will be quickly and correctly serviced. After you have been repping for several months, you should begin to build up a picture of how well different types of books sell in each of the shops you visit.

Of most interest to the buyer will be news of forthcoming titles or 'frontlist'. Selling these forthcoming books into shops is known as subscribing. Booksellers know that they will benefit most from having these titles for sale on publication when your publicity appears and creates a readership.

Ensure each title has a definite publication date. Although the tradition of not selling prior to publication is no longer as rigorously observed as in the past, it may prevent shops that receive their stocks earliest in an area from scooping the bulk of the trade and thus upsetting your other stockists.

When subscribing titles, you can offer to take down orders in your own order book. However, you may find that many booksellers will prefer to use their own order forms so that they can keep a duplicate on file for their records. Others will not give you the orders at all but arrange for them to be forwarded on to you via 'Teleordering' (see below).

Always bear in mind that you may be able to sell some titles to several departments in larger shops. For example, a biography of a famous actress might be sold into the cinema/theatre and biography departments and into a women's section.

If it is your first meeting with a buyer, be sure to lead with the titles of most interest. Most reps carry only the covers/jackets of forthcoming titles in a plastic display folder together with a copy of the Advance Information sheet (see Chapter 2). Backlist titles can usually be repped adequately from your catalogue. You may find it useful to take in the publications themselves, if finished copies are available, if you are a new publisher or have illustrated or unusual titles.

Keep notes on the specialities of each shop or department and the reactions you receive from each buyer. Consult these before your next visit. Selling books is much like selling any other product and building up a good relationship with the buyer is an important key to success.

On future visits, check the bookshop's shelves to see whether the titles you repped in previously have sold out. If they have, ask the buyer whether further copies are required and if possible take a re-order.

Obtaining sufficient re-orders for your titles is a perpetual headache, and particularly so for the new publisher whose titles may not have obvious commercial appeal. Many shops operate stock control systems which, they claim, automatically trigger re-orders when a title reaches a particular stock level. These rarely work to the liking of reps but it is difficult to persuade shops to re-order when you visit unless the book has a new burst of publicity or has an established track record. Try nevertheless.

All this can be very frustrating to publishers who feel that there would be a demand for their books if only shops would stock them! Remember that around 50,000 new titles plus many re-issues are published in Britain each year, so buyers do have to be selective.

If you are collecting orders which will not be supplied immediately (for example because the title is reprinting), tell the buyer this when the order is placed just as you would for a title not yet published.

An enthusiastic and down-to-earth approach helps when selling new titles but remember that the major concern of commercial booksellers is whether a title will sell and whether the terms are right. Standard terms for bookshops to buy at are from 33 to 35 per cent discount of the retail price, although mass-market paperback discounts are frequently higher. Except in special circumstances, no bookseller will be willing to subscribe your titles at lower discounts than these and certain chains will demand higher ones. Carriage charges involved in getting the books from your warehouse to bookshops within the UK are nearly always paid by the publisher/distributor, although some publishers charge carriage on low value orders.

Unless other arrangements have been made, most booksellers are expected to pay their bills within 30 days of the statement they should receive from suppliers at the end of each month. Perhaps not surprisingly, many will stretch their credit period for longer and publishers should keep a watchful eye on the state of their customers' accounts if they are supplying direct rather than via a distributor. It can play havoc with your own cash flow plans if payments don't come in when expected.

Specialist and community bookshops will also judge titles by the message they promulgate; they want to buy and sell the titles that are within their field of commitment. They expect and should receive the same sort of terms and treatment that you give to general high street stores.

You should also find out what procedures each shop uses for the payment of invoices and what documentation is required. Most independent bookshops will be quite happy with an invoice delivered with the goods, but most of the chains have central accounting departments to which invoices should be sent. Of course, if you are using a distributor, they should already be aware of most booksellers' requirements.

When selling to shops with which you have not opened account facilities, it is normal practice to issue a pro-forma invoice until you get a clear indication of the likely value of future business.

Order Consolidation
There are a number of companies that provide a link between booksellers and publishers by consolidating orders. All new publishers are advised to provide these organisations with full details of their distribution arrangements.

Teleordering is a limited company set up in 1979 to facilitate the transmission of orders from booksellers to publishers. Most large publishers, booksellers and distributors are subscribers to the Teleordering system which allows booksellers to transmit orders electronically to publishers much more quickly than through the mail.

If you do not subscribe to Teleordering – and it is expensive for the small publisher – you can still benefit to an extent from the service they provide. Orders transmitted through the system are consolidated and will then be forwarded to you by mail. Of course, understandably, neither Teleordering nor their subscribing members are very happy with this situation and it is always possible that they may bring an end to it. For further information, contact Teleordering Ltd (see Addresses).

Orders Clearing is a department of IBIS Information Services (see Addresses) who are perhaps best known to publishers as a mailing house offering list rental services. However, they also operate an orders clearing facility, consolidating publishers orders from a variety of different bookshops around the country.

BOD: Order Distribution (see Addresses). This company provides an order consolidation service enabling booksellers to route all their orders through one channel. Orders are then batched by BOD and forwarded to the various publishers/distributors.

Terms of Supply

It is important to be aware of the terms of ordering prevalent in the booktrade. These are standard terms used throughout the whole trade but some booksellers and publishers interpret them in different ways.

Firm Orders Expect all orders to be firm unless otherwise agreed. This means that the bookseller should pay for them within an agreed period and not return them for credit without prior permission from the publisher. In certain rare circumstances, it can also be interpreted as meaning that the books purchased are non-returnable, but this is extremely unlikely unless very substantial discounts have been offered.

See Safe This means that books are supplied to the shop and charged to the account but may be returned within a specified period without prior permission. This may work well for new publishers trying to get their books into reluctant outlets.

Sale or Return This is to be avoided unless you are totally stuck. In this case, books are supplied to the shop but not charged until copies are sold or at the end of an agreed period. During this period, the shop can return the stock and no charge can be made. There are one or two publishers who specialise in this form of supply and, although it is generally not recommended, it can work for specialist publishers trying to break into non-traditional outlets where books are not a major priority of the business.

Book Trade Discounts

If you intend selling a significant quantity of titles through the book trade, careful thought will have to be given to the complex area of trade discounts at an early stage in the publishing process. The size of discount you offer to the trade will have a considerable effect on your profit margins and will therefore greatly influence your pricing policy (see Chapter 2).

It is difficult to generalise on the subject of discounts, because much will depend on the type of titles you publish and the demands of the outlets to be supplied. The number of units ordered at any one time, or their value, may also be factors affecting what you offer. A good starting point in establishing a discount policy is to find out what comparable publishers give. Check out their catalogues or refer to the *Directory of Book Publishers, Distributors and Wholesalers* (see Bibliography) which details terms of supply.

As a basic rule, it is reasonable to assume that retailers will not subscribe general titles for stock at less than 35 per cent discount. Some specialist shops and branches of major chains may well ask for more and are unlikely to consider taking stock if their terms are not met. (See section on major retail outlets, above, for further details.)

Wholesalers buying stock for selling on to retail outlets will be looking for much higher discounts and if you are publishing books likely to appeal to the wholesale trade, expect to give 50 per cent. Similar discounts will be required by W H Smith and John Menzies when they buy stock centrally for 'scaling out' to their many branches. Sales into airport bookshops come at an even higher premium, with discounts of 57.5 per cent being standard.

Many publishers penalise booksellers who order single copies of titles, or whose orders do not meet a minimum value requirement. This is usually done in the form of a 'small order surcharge' or by giving less discount – for instance 25 per cent. Although not popular with the trade it may be the only way to keep your costs at a reasonable level.

Non-traditional Outlets

There are an increasing number of outlets outside of the general book trade, in addition to CTNs, supermarkets and department stores, which now sell books alongside a variety of other goods. Many of them are unlikely to be visited by general trade representatives and accordingly tend to purchase stock from wholesalers or select titles that have come to their attention through other sources.

Among these are wholefood shops which often stock a range of cookery and green interest titles. However, there are many others covering such areas as local history, photography, music, art, new age, etc. Specialist shops can move large quantities of books and should not be ignored if you want to maximise your sales.

If you are publishing in subject areas likely to be of interest to such outlets, it is important that you alert your reps to their existence and see if they can arrange to visit them. This may not be possible, and if this is the case, you should let them know that you intend to cover such outlets through another agency or contact them direct. Such arrangements are not unusual and your agency will be very unlikely to demand commission on sales generated.

As with selling to booksellers, the personal visit is the best method of approach. However, if this is not convenient, send your Advance Information material to the shops along with a cover and follow this up with a phone call. Many specialist outlets pay much more attention to information received through the mail than general bookshops as they want to ensure that they have comprehensive coverage of their area of interest.

Trade Press

In addition to ensuring each new title is listed in the bibliographic sections of the trade press, you may want to consider trying to get editorial coverage in *The Bookseller* and other trade periodicals. It is not difficult to place pieces in the Publicity and Promotion column of *The Bookseller*, which is read by the vast majority of booksellers. *The Radical Bookseller* also offers coverage to appropriate titles and both publications accept advertising. Some of the larger chains, such as Waterstones, also produce their own lists of titles for their customers' use and it may be worth contacting them if you feel you have a suitable title.

Many small publishers confine their trade advertising to the twice yearly special issues of *The Bookseller* in which they announce their forthcoming titles. Editorial entries can also be placed in these special editions. If you do advertise in the weekly issues, the advertisements should ideally appear just before the representatives subscribe the title. Current theories of what is effective copy are evident in the ads. The longest surviving effective ingredient is probably humour. Advance coverage in *The Bookseller* will sometimes lead to a title being picked up by literary and features editors for coverage in the press. It can also stimulate rights sales and export business.

It is also important to keep the appropriate sections of *The Bookseller* informed of activities that are likely to be of interest to the trade. This should include details of your distribution or repping arrangements, major publicity events and any changes in key personnel. They also carry an occasional independent publishers column which often features information on new imprints and publications.

Promoting Through Retail Outlets

Retail outlets provide obvious opportunities for a variety of special displays. Have a look in your local bookshop to get an idea of the kinds of display material produced by larger publishers.

The simplest method of drawing attention to your title is the show card. This can be easily produced in-house by mounting a poster or a spare dust jacket on a large (A3, usually) piece of stout but lightweight coloured card. Be sure to include the price and month of publication in bold lettering. Show cards can be used in window displays as well as in store. As with all display material, it is important to ensure that the production quality is of a high standard.

Certain titles – in particular those with impulse-buying potential – may best be displayed in counter packs. These custom built cardboard 'trays' usually hold about a dozen copies. They are ideally placed next to the cash point in key outlets.

Next up the scale comes the 'dump bin'. These free-standing showcases, generally used by paperback publishers to promote a lead title or series, will hold around 48 copies in 12 compartments. With an appropriate header board this method of display can be particularly eyecatching.

More ambitiously, a 'spinner' will ensure your list is given maximum exposure. These revolving plastic stands can hold 150 or more copies of a variety of titles from your list. They may be mounted either on the floor or a table.

Special display units are usually expensive to manufacture and for this reason are used predominantly by larger publishing houses. However, some smaller specialist publishers do use them successfully in appropriate outlets. As shop-floor space is at a premium in most retail outlets approach shops first before committing yourself to heavy expenditure or you may find yourself with an office full of junk. It is important to ensure the name of your imprint appears prominently on all display material. This is not only good advertising, it will also dissuade shops from using it to promote other publishers' lists. Probably the main supplier of in-store display material for the book trade in the UK is Point Eight (see Addresses).

Given the number of new titles published in Britain each year, the competition to promote an individual title – especially in general bookshops – is fierce. You may find that, although smaller independent bookshops and shops specialising in the subject area will be prepared to devote valuable space to displaying your material, the larger, more style-conscious stores are less likely to be interested.

If, however, you think you deserve a window display in a branch of Waterstones, or an in-store display in W H Smith to promote the work of a local author, ask to speak to the shop manager or display manager and be persuasive but polite. If possible, link an intended bookshop promotion in with an appropriate local or national event. You will have to supply the back-up publicity and you may also have to agree to supply the stock on sale or return or at a higher discount. Before agreeing to any special terms, be sure to advise your distributor and reps.

Other Methods of Promoting and Selling to the Trade

In his book *Sales on a Shoestring, How to Advertise Books* (André Deutsch, 1956, now out of print), Sydney Hyde recounts a stunt put on for both the trade and public when Ronald Searle's *The Terrors of St Trinians* was published:

> On this occasion Miss Hermione Gingold, dressed in the well-known St Trinians uniform, arrived on the roof of a taxi-cab outside the premises of a well-known bookshop. After a certain amount of altercation, which speedily caused a considerable crowd to collect, she hurled a brick through the bookshop window to the general consternation of the spectators, and to very great effect. Not only was the glass window well and truly broken but attention became focussed on the array of copies of the book which the window had been dressed with. The press no doubt had been well primed for the event, for photographs were included in almost all the evening papers and a good deal of editorial publicity resulted. Once again, the trade was amused by the incident, talked about it and from that moment always had the book in mind.

Such high jinks may not be the fare of small publishers if it costs a plate glass window, but some titles will present the option of a stunt or publicity event of interest to the press.

Selling to the trade by the post and by telephone is also worth considering but can only be done effectively once your list is known. Opinion varies on the effectiveness of these methods. Some publishers have developed a feel for them. You need to have built up a relationship with the buyer before you can expect any success.

Trade Promotions

Trade promotions are organised with the aim of promoting books with a particular theme. They can be a good way for specialist publishers or those with appropriately thematic titles to bring their publications to the attention of a wide range of booksellers and librarians. Usually held annually, these promotions are organised by various bodies eager to increase public awareness of their specific subject interest.

In most cases, publishers submit books to the organising body who then shortlist titles to be highlighted during the promotion. Such events usually run for a week or two and are accompanied by an intensive publicity campaign involving window displays, signings, readings etc. Many of the major promotions are supported by the large wholesalers and chains and there can be opportunities to shift a large volume of books.

The Bookseller is perhaps the best place to watch out for promotions that might be appropriate for you, but two well established ones are:

Children's Book Week Held in October, details from the Children's Book Foundation (see Addresses).

Feminist Book Fortnight Held in June, details from FBF (see Addresses).

6

Representation and Distribution

If it is your intention to sell books through the book trade, it is most important that you make arrangements for trade representation and distribution prior to finalising your publishing plans. Surprisingly, some new publishers embark on publishing programmes without giving a thought to how they are going to sell and distribute their titles. This can be a recipe for disaster.

Do not underestimate the amount of work involved in selling and distributing your publications. It is often impossible for publishers to find the time or financial resources to handle this aspect of their work themselves and most therefore contract out much of it to companies which specialise in providing such services.

You may find one company that will handle both sales and distribution or alternatively you can contract them out separately. Which course of action you decide on will depend to a large extent on the size and nature of your list. Be aware, however, that you may have difficulty in finding a company to handle distribution alone unless your turnover is reasonably significant.

Making Arrangements for Representation

On the assumption that you will not have the financial ability to hire your own sales force, there is a range of possibilities open to you in this area:

- Doing it yourself.
- Working with a specialist repping agency.
- Using individual freelance representatives.
- Making an arrangement with a combined repping and distribution company.
- Combining your list with that of another larger publisher who have their own sales force.

Doing your own repping may be a suitable choice for the small specialist publisher with a limited range of potential outlets. If you are confident that the number of shops which will be prepared to take stock of your products is small enough for you to cover easily and efficiently yourself by personal calls and by phone, then this may be your best bet. As the publisher, you will probably subscribe more copies than someone less directly involved with your list and you will get to know the buyers first hand.

If, on the other hand, the shops you need to call on are spread nationwide, or the potential is too great for you to handle alone, then this method of selling will prove impractical and you will have to consider one of the other options.

Making the best choice for your list needs careful consideration. It is likely that your chosen representatives or agents will require you to sign a twelve month contract – a long time to wait for a change if you feel unhappy with the service provided. Try contacting other publishers active in your field for advice. They will usually be happy to give you recommendations based on their own experience. You can also speak to local booksellers or refer to the *Book Publishers' Representatives' Handbook*. This is available from the BPRA (see Addresses).

You will need to look carefully at the costs of the service on offer. Most agencies and freelancers charge a percentage of net area sales which is usually in the region of 10–12.5 per cent. This means that commission paid will be based on total trade sales in the territory, not just on orders made via the reps. You may be able to negotiate a lower rate for sales to library suppliers, wholesalers or chains which buy in bulk at higher discounts, but this is by no means guaranteed. Some agencies will also ask for a lump sum as a signing-on fee or an annual premium payment as well. When you pay your agency is a matter of agreement but most will expect payment within 30 to 60 days of the month of sale. This may prove difficult during your first two or three months of trading and you should take this into account when negotiating a contract.

Whichever you select, your agents will expect a proper briefing on your publishing plans and will need to feel confident that your books are going to appear on schedule.

Representatives can only work effectively if they have some enthusiasm for the product they are selling. Make sure you attend sales meetings whenever possible and be prepared to brief your reps fully on forthcoming titles. They will want to know what publicity you have planned, what readership you are aiming for and each title's key selling points. Try to get an idea of how many copies they expect to subscribe and solicit their views on pricing, format and cover design. Expect honest criticism!

Most reps will want two to three months to show a new title to all their outlets. Accurate publication schedules, Advance Information sheets (see Glossary) and attractive covers will help them in their task. Visual material is all important and they will expect you to have covers available for the beginning of their repping cycle. If this is difficult, a photocopy of the cover artwork will sometimes suffice while the cover is in production. Remember, your book will be competing with others in their folder and it is likely that they will put the most effort into those that are easiest to present and promise the best return.

Some points to consider when making a repping arrangement with an agency:

- How many representatives do they have?
- How often do they visit the areas you want covered?
- How many titles do they carry?
- Would they do your titles justice?
- Do they visit all appropriate types of bookshop?
- Do they sell to other outlets (such as library suppliers)?
- What kind of contact would you have with the reps?
- Can they provide you with regular travel itineraries?
- Do they circulate catalogues or other promotion material?
- How will they report on their activities?
- How much would they charge?
- Will you pay them on orders which come from the territory but which they did not raise directly?
- Are they asking for an exclusive deal or can you use other agents as well?
- Is VAT payable?
- How quickly would you have to pay them?
- What is the notice period of the agreement?

An example of an agreement between a publisher and a repping agency is given in Figure 6.1.

Making a Distribution Arrangement

Although you may decide to handle your own mail order distribution, it is likely that sooner or later you will require the services of a distributor if your list is to be marketed effectively to booksellers and library suppliers. Apart from the obvious economies in cost of combining your list with that of other publishers, you will find that booksellers are becoming increasingly resistant to maintaining accounts with small publishers and will be more willing to stock your titles if they can be supplied and invoiced by one of the recognised trade distributors.

Distribution work ranges from warehousing of stock through invoicing, dispatch and collecting payment to compiling sales statistics. Historically seen by many publishers as the least important part of their activities, it is now taken very seriously and acknowledged as a vital part of the marketing process. Most booksellers are no longer willing

Figure 6.1 Sample agreement Between Publisher and Sales Representative

Memorandum of Agreement

Between: Bloggs Books Ltd (hereinafter referred to as 'the Publisher')
    1 High Street
    Anytown AN3 3BB

and: Ace Repping Ltd (hereinafter referred to as 'the Representative')
    2 High Street
    Othertown OT3 3BB

Whereby it is agreed that:

1. The Publisher appoints the Representative to be the sole booktrade representative of their product in the following territories: England, Scotland, Wales and the Channel Islands.

2. The commencement date of the agreement shall be: 1 January 1994.

3. The agreement shall be for an initial period of twelve months and thereafter until terminated by either party giving three months' notice in writing.

4. On all orders from the territories, invoiced by the Publisher, or appointed distributor, the Publisher will pay the Representative 10% of the invoice value as commission – excluding any taxes or transportation charges.

5. The Publisher reserves the right to refrain from executing any order and also to set a limit at any time on the amount of credit allowed any individual account.

6. The Publisher will provide the Representative with sales figures, by account, for the territory within 30 days of the end of each month.

7. On receipt of monthly sales figures, the Representative will raise an invoice to the Publisher for the commission due plus VAT. The Publisher undertakes to pay this invoice within 30 days of the end of the month of issue.

8. The Publisher will send – free of charge – appropriate promotion and publicity material to the Representative on a regular basis.

9. The Publisher will supply the Representative with 4 (four) free copies of each new title prior to publication.

10. The Representative will provide the Publisher with a schedule of visits to key accounts within the territory on a quarterly basis.

11. The Representative undertakes to visit and subscribe all appropriate titles to key accounts in the territory and forward all orders for new and backlist titles to the Publisher for supply.

12. The Representative undertakes to attend quarterly sales meetings held by the Publisher.

13. Any additional services not covered by this agreement shall be undertaken by the Representative only by prior agreement with the Publisher at a mutually agreed rate.

14. In the event of termination of this agreement by either party, commission shall be paid up to the date at which the agreement ceases.

to carry multiple copies of what may be slow moving titles and expect publishers to be able to provide them with a rapid turn round of orders to meet their customers' demands. Publishers, too, are evermore aware of the need to monitor sales performance and stock holdings; regular reports from distributors are an integral part of this process.

As with representation, one of the best ways of finding a distributor is to find out who like-minded publishers use. Again, talk to publishers active in your field and to booksellers, who will often have a much better overview of the efficiency of the distributors under consideration. Bear in mind that few booksellers have a good word to say about distributors and a cross-section of opinion is essential. The Booksellers Association *Directory of Book Publishers, Distributors and Wholesalers* and book fairs, such as the London International Book Fair, may prove useful ways of finding out what is available. Appendix 2, Addresses, lists a selection of distributors working for small and independent publishers.

When choosing a distributor, you may find your options are limited. Many of the larger companies will not consider publishers with an annual turnover of less than £150,000 per annum and unless you can convince them of your future growth potential it is unlikely that they will be willing to take on your list. Of course, it may be possible to find a friendly larger publisher who can include you on their contract but it is more likely that you will have to consider a smaller distributor or one offering a combined repping and distribution service. Do not be put off. It may well be much better than having your books 'lost' in a large operation and costs and efficiency are unlikely to differ significantly.

Distributors' charges are normally based on a percentage of net turnover, usually between 10 and 14 per cent. In addition, you will be charged carriage costs for dispatch, usually 4–6 per cent. Charges for the service, plus VAT, will be deducted at source by the distributor and the balance owing from sales will be paid over to you after an agreed credit period. For UK sales, this will usually be between 60 and 90 days after the month of sale but on export orders can be as much as 120 days. It is likely that you will be responsible for any bad debts incurred by customers failing to pay for the supplies of your books.

Some distributors offering a combined repping and distribution service base their charges on retail prices. In such cases, distributors will take in the region of 55 per cent of the retail price of each book sold. This usually works out much the same costwise as separate arrangements but all the activities will be covered by a single contract.

Distributors will expect you to arrange delivery of stock to their warehouse in advance of the publication date. Stock is normally held on a consignment basis – that is, it remains the property of the publisher until sold.

When choosing a distributor, consider such issues as:

- How much do they charge?
- On what do they base their charges?
- How long a credit period are they asking for?
- Is warehousing of bulk stock offered?
- To whom does the stock belong?
- Who pays carriage on deliveries and how is it calculated?
- Who is responsible for insuring the stock?
- Who pays for transport from printer/publisher to distributor's warehouse?
- How long do they take to service orders?
- Will you be required to forward all orders to them?
- Can they cope at busy times?
- Is there a minimum acceptable turnover?
- Can they cope with your discount structure?
- What sales information will they provide?
- How efficient is their invoicing, dispatch and cash collection?
- Who bears bad debts?
- Is VAT payable?
- Who are their other clients?
- Are there benefits to be gained from forming a consortium of publishers to use their service?
- What is the notice period in the agreement?

It is impossible to give norms in these matters, so make comparisons between offers from various distributors.

You will also need to obtain at least two trade references and/or bank references to check up on the distributor's reliability, particularly in the area of payment. Ask the distributor to supply names and addresses for these. If they are trade references, you should approach the referees direct. If they are bank references, you will need to ask your own bank to approach their bank on your behalf. Some larger distributors hold the money owing to their client publishers in separate bank accounts to the distributor's own funds. Check whether this is an option as it may offer you some protection.

A typical example of an agreement between a publisher and distribution company is given in Figure 6.2.

Handling Your Own Invoicing

Another way of dealing with the invoicing and distribution of your orders is to contract out the physical picking, packing and dispatch of goods to a distributor, retaining the invoicing in house. This arrangement will require you to run a full invoicing and sales ledger system,

Figure 6.2 Sample Agreement Between Publisher and Distributor

Memorandum of Agreement

Between: Bloggs Books Ltd (hereinafter referred to as 'the Publisher')
            1 High Street
            Anytown AN3 3BB

and: Ace Distribution Ltd (hereinafter referred to as 'the Distributor')
            3 High Street
            Othertown OT3 3BB

Whereby it is mutually agreed as follows concerning distribution of the Publisher's titles by the Distributor.

1. The Publisher appoints the Distributor as the sole trade distributor of the Publisher's titles throughout the following territories: UK and Ireland.

2. The Publisher agrees to indemnify the Distributor against all damages, costs, charges or expenses to which the Distributor may become liable arising out of any actionable matter in any publications held or sold by the Distributor.

3. The Publisher undertakes to advise the Distributor of the delivery of stock of new titles and to ensure that such deliveries are made at a time convenient to both parties. All costs, insurance and any other expenses incurred in deliveries to the Distributor's warehouse shall be borne by the Publisher.

4. The Publisher agrees to provide the Distributor with full bibliographical information on forthcoming titles at least three months prior to publication and any changes to availability or price of backlist titles.

5. The Publisher agrees to forward all trade orders received from the territory to the Distributor for supply.

6. The Distributor agrees to hold and warehouse all the Publisher's stock in a secure manner. The Distributor undertakes to maintain at its expense adequate insurance covering damage, destruction, theft or loss of publications held on its premises.

7. The Distributor undertakes to invoice and dispatch all trade orders received for available titles within 5 working days of receipt.

8. The Distributor undertakes to process all returns received on behalf of the Publisher and raise appropriate credit notes.

9. The Distributor will maintain records of all sales ledger transactions and issue statements to all trade accounts on a monthly basis.

10. The Distributor will maintain all proper books of accounts showing all sums of money received in respect of sales transactions and shall pay to the Publisher a sum equal to the net value of all invoices and credits raised on behalf of the Publisher less the charges defined in Clause 15 on or before the expiration of 90 days of the end of the calendar month in which the transactions were made.

11. The Distributor undertakes to hold all monies received on behalf of the Publisher in a separate Publishers' account and such monies will be legally owned by the Publisher and not viewed as an asset of the Distributor.

12. The Distributor reserves the right not to supply any customers viewed by the Distributor to be an unacceptable credit risk unless requested in writing by the Publisher in which case the Distributor will not be held responsible for any resulting outstanding debts.

13. Debts arising as a result of any transaction carried out on behalf of the Publisher which remain uncollected within 90 days of the date payment relating to the transaction was made to the Publisher shall be passed back to the Publisher provided that all normal collection procedures have been exhausted.

14. Within five working days of the end of each month, the Distributor will provide the Publisher with:
    (a) a statement of all stocks held, sales and returns processed.
    (b) a statement analysing sales by turnover of each account supplied.
    (c) a list of outstanding orders for all forthcoming titles and titles out of stock or reprinting.

15. For the services provided, the Publisher undertakes to pay the Distributor:
    (a) a commission of 10.5% of sales invoiced.
    (b) a commission of 10.5% of credit note value in the event of credits raised exceeding 5% of sales invoiced in any twelve-month period.
    (c) postage and carriage charges for the dispatch of goods at a rate of 4% of net invoice value with a minimum charge per dispatch of £1.75.
    (d) bulk storage charges at a rate of £7.00 per 1,000 units per month where stocks of a title held are in excess of twice the units sold in the previous 24-month period.
    (e) stickering costs at a rate of £7.50 per 100 units.
    (f) for the dispatch of gratis copies at a rate of 50p per copy plus carriage.

    Any services provided by the Distributor at the request of the Publisher shall be charged at a rate to be mutually agreed.

    All charges are exclusive of VAT.

16. All charges covered in this Agreement shall be reviewed annually and may be altered with effect from 1 April following the commencement of the Agreement. The rate of commission charged may only be altered if the trading activities of the Publisher have changed so substantially from the date of the Agreement as to be detrimental to the Distributor.

17. All books held by the Distributor on behalf of the Publisher are the property of the Publisher and may be inspected by the Publisher providing reasonable notice is given.

18. At the end of each financial year, the Distributor will carry out a stocktake of the Publisher's titles and provide the Publisher with a list of stock held.

19. This Agreement shall commence on 1 January 1994 and continue for a period of twelve months and thereafter until terminated by either party giving three months' notice in writing.

20. In the event of the termination of this Agreement, costs for the removal and transfer of the Publisher's stock will be borne by the party giving notice of termination.

including the dispatch of monthly statements to bookshops, cash collection and credit control. Although you will have peace of mind that all financial matters are under your control, it will of course involve you in considerable extra work which you may not have the resources or expertise to handle.

Liaison with Representatives and Distributors

We have already mentioned the importance of keeping your representatives up-to-date on your publishing plans and promotion. It is also important to keep them informed of progress. Tell them about any publicity which will help them to convince booksellers that there will be a demand for your titles. For example, inform them as early as possible of any media coverage you expect to receive and send them copies of reviews as soon as they come out.

It is little use the publisher being convinced of the value of a new title if their representatives are not. Talk to them about it and try and communicate some of your enthusiasm.

It is unwise to spend too long in publishing without actually getting out to the bookshops with a rep. Ask your representatives if you can join them for a day or two visiting shops.

Stick to publication dates and deadlines. Your distributor cannot be expected to make up your slippage. Their credibility will suffer along with yours if your early publicity information is not reasonably accurate.

Fix realistic payment arrangements. Do not hesitate to check with other publishers who use the same distributor to see that they are satisfied and that agreed payment terms are honoured.

If you are unhappy with the service your distributor or representatives are giving you, complain to them. There may be ways that you can get together and improve the situation. But it is realistic to remember that your titles are competing with the other lists they handle.

Stock Transport

Once your books are printed, you will most likely be faced with the task of transporting stock to one or more locations. The initial transfer of stock from your printer to your primary storage location will usually be made as part of the agreed printing costs. Some printers are prepared to make other deliveries on your behalf but this will incur additional charges. If you are using a trade distributor, or storage company, you may find it cheaper to transfer all your stock there along with instructions for onward forwarding. Such companies are normally familiar with the options for both domestic and overseas transportation and will be happy to arrange this on your behalf.

Making your own arrangements for bulk transportation may prove problematic and expensive so tread carefully. A good source of carriers specialising in book transport is the annual London International Book Fair catalogue (see the section on Book Fairs); identify which companies may be suitable and ask for quotes. Alternatively, your printer or other publishers may be able to offer advice. If your books are going to an overseas distributor, they may well have an arrangement with a forwarder in the UK, or again, may be able to offer advice. Finally, depending on the volume of books to be transported and the destination, you may find the Post Office's parcel service worth considering.

7

Reaching Libraries and the Specialist Market

Libraries

Library expenditure on books makes up a significant proportion of the UK book market (some estimates go as high as 10 per cent of value) and practically all publishers – large or small – should give serious attention to ensuring that their titles are well represented within it.

Estimated figures for 1989/90 show public libraries buying over £90 million of books with libraries in educational establishments spending some £143 million (source: Euromonitor). All in all, approximately 14 per cent of books sold in the UK go to libraries.

Although libraries are likely to prove an important purchasing sector for your titles, you should not deceive yourself that everyone uses them. It has been estimated that 65 per cent of the public never borrow books from a library and some 70 per cent never use the reference facilities. Still, given that libraries in the UK made approximately 583 million loans in 1990, it does suggest that those who use them do so very regularly. Furthermore, Euromonitor's report for 1991 estimates that 32 per cent of books obtained in the UK are borrowed from libraries.

How Do Libraries Select Books?
If you want to sell your books into libraries, it is a good idea to have a grasp of how libraries select which titles they will stock. No two libraries are likely to operate in exactly the same way, but we can make some useful generalisations.

Academic Libraries
Most titles stocked in such libraries are purchased on the recommendations of faculty academics, usually as a result of being on course reading lists. Other titles, however, are chosen by librarians who have responsibility for selecting titles within the various subject areas covered.

Librarians find out about suitable titles from a variety of sources. These include:

- publishers' leaflets and catalogues;
- the *British National Bibliography* and Cataloguing in Publication;
- reviews and advertisements in journals;
- bibliographical listings in periodicals;
- word of mouth.

Books are purchased from general library suppliers and specialist academic retailers such as Blackwells in Oxford, Heffers in Cambridge and John Smith in Glasgow. Many libraries will also place orders with publishers direct.

Professional Libraries

Many organisations in both the public and private sector run specialist libraries. These can range from research libraries in large companies to smaller libraries on specific issues within governmental establishments, professional associations and a wide variety of voluntary organisations and charities. It is difficult to quantify the volume of publications purchased by such libraries, but if you have a title which has an obvious market in this sector it will be worth considering including them in your publicity mailings. Addresses can be derived from a variety of sources such as a mailing list broker (see Chapter 3), the Directory of British Associations or the NCVO Directory of Voluntary Organisations. There are many other directories of organisations available and a trip to your local reference library may be productive. There are also a number of booksellers who target their activities to these types of libraries.

Public Libraries

These libraries serve the local community and librarians select titles for them on the basis of what they perceive as being actual or likely demand.

They find out about titles from:

- library suppliers (see below);
- local booksellers;
- press reviews;
- publishers' catalogues;
- publications such as *The Bookseller* and the *British National Bibliography*.

Occasionally, they will also visit the major library suppliers' showrooms and make selections from what is on display.

Both public and academic librarians will also have access to records indicating what books and what type of books are in local demand and have a good idea what their borrowers want to read. Since the introduction of Public Lending Rights in 1979, general information on national borrowing trends has been widely available to librarians and publishers alike.

Public Library Purchasing Policy

Most public library authorities have a policy that specifies how they will obtain various categories of books. The majority place most of their business with the few large library suppliers, but a certain amount of business is often placed with local bookshops, thus supporting local trade. Historically, the local shop has been a useful source for books produced by small publishers which were not readily on offer from the larger suppliers. However, increased competition for diminishing local library authority budgets has led the larger suppliers to show a greater interest in the smaller houses in an effort to provide a comprehensive service.

To a limited extent publishers can also sell direct to public libraries and to a larger extent to libraries at colleges of further education. However, most libraries prefer to order from a specialist supplier who will look after their own particular ticketing and jacketing requirements as part of the service.

Hardbacks or Paperbacks?

The decline in local authority spending over the last decade has led to changes in the policy of many local library authorities. Long gone are the days when they automatically purchased hardback editions and paperbacks now make up a significant amount of most library budgets.

This does not mean that you should dismiss the ideas of publishing a hardback edition, but a careful marketing decision needs to be made. Much will depend on the type of book under consideration. Is it aimed predominantly at the library market or at individual purchasers? A novel by an established author, for example, which a library will expect to lend frequently, may well find a ready hardback market. On the other hand, a topical guide or handbook which may date quickly will perhaps be preferred in paper.

Many publishers bind up a small part of their print-runs in hardback – perhaps 300 copies – specifically for the library market and manage to recuperate a considerable proportion of their investment on these more profitable editions. It is worth considering this option but unless you feel confident that libraries will prefer your books in hardback it may be safer to stick with a paperback edition. If in doubt, visit some libraries to see what the competition is doing and talk to a librarian or library supplier.

Of course, there are factors other than the library market to consider when deciding whether to publish in hardback or paper. You may want to publish a hardback edition under your own imprint and sell paperback rights to another publisher (see Chapter 9).

Finally, it is worth noting that libraries abhor printing on the inside of covers.

Library Suppliers

Library suppliers bring books to the attention of their customers by supplying them with regular 'on approval' copies of new titles and/or detailed bibliographical listings. Approval copies are usually displayed centrally for viewing by branch and reference librarians, and orders are then placed with the various suppliers.

These suppliers can order substantial quantities of books for these 'on approval' schemes but will insist on the option to return unsold copies which may not always be in mint condition. In general, they will ask for discounts of 35–40 per cent of which they will pass on 10 per cent to the purchasing libraries. Payment terms vary from supplier to supplier but many will expect 90 days credit.

If you plan to publish several titles of interest to libraries, visiting the major suppliers to meet the relevant people will help you understand their requirements. If you are using representatives to sell your books, make sure they call on the large suppliers to subscribe your titles to those operating approval services.

The Major Suppliers The major suppliers control a large proportion of the library market – indeed seven suppliers control some 90 per cent of it – and if you want to sell substantial quantities of books to them, it is essential that you fit in with their requirements. This needs careful advance planning. Remember that they are dealing with hundreds of books every week and if you fail to comply with their procedures, they are unlikely to be sympathetic to your list.

The big seven are:

- James Askew & Son, 218–222 North Road, Preston, Lancs PR1 1SY. Tel: 0772 555947. Also handle British Council book orders. Send one cover and one AI for each title plus catalogues.
- Books for Students, Bird Road, Heathcote, Warks CV34 6TB. Tel: 0926 314366. Mostly paperbacks and cover all subjects. Strong in school supply. Send one cover and one AI for each title plus catalogues.
- T C Farries & Co, Irongray Road, Lochside, Dumfries DG2 0LH. Tel: 0387 720755. Send one cover and one AI for each title plus catalogues.
- Holt Jackson Book Co, Preston Road, Lytham, Lancs FY8 5AX. Tel: 0253 737464. Send one AI for each title plus 70 covers for each non-fiction title and catalogues.

- JMLS Ltd, Gamble Street, Nottingham NG7 4FJ. Tel: 0602 708021. Send 60 covers and two AIs for each new trade, fiction and children's title plus four copies of each catalogue.
- Morley Book Company, Elmfield Road, Morley, Leeds LS27 0NN. Tel: 0532 538811. Send one cover and one AI for each title plus catalogues.
- Woodfield & Stanley, Broad Lane, Moldgreen, Huddersfield HD5 8DD. Tel: 0484 21467. Specialise in children's and educational books. Send one cover and one AI for each title.

Between three and six months prior to publication, you will need to send out an Advance Information sheet to these suppliers for the attention of the Bibliographic Services Department. Give all the details, even if they are not firm.

Follow this up two to three months before publication with advance jackets (or covers if paperback); one of each unless specified otherwise in the list above. For selected titles, it may also be worth supplying a finished copy in advance of publication.

The list is by no means definitive and their take-up of your books will depend very much on the material you publish. However, it should provide a useful starting point for your entry into this market.

Some will order bulk copies on approval while others will only order in response to their client libraries.

There are a number of other suppliers – large and small – who it will be worth keeping informed of your forthcoming titles. Some of these operate in specialist areas so it is worth contacting them prior to adding them to your mailing list to receive one AI plus catalogues unless otherwise stated. They include:

- Albany Book Company, 30 Clydeholm Road, Glasgow G14 0BJ. Tel: 041 954 2271. Send two covers and two AIs for each title.
- Allied Libraries, Craven Road, Altrincham, Cheshire W14 5HJ. Tel: 061 928 9326.
- BH Blackwell, NEBS Dept, Beaver House, Hythe Bridge Street, Oxford OX1 2ET. Tel: 0865 792792. Specialise in exporting British books.
- Bookscan, Unit 9, Angela Davis Industrial Estate, Somerleyton Road, London SW9 8TZ. Tel: 071 274 6499. Particularly supportive of small publishers.
- Burchell and Martin, 34 Granville Street, Birmingham B1 2LJ. Tel: 021 643 1888.
- Collets Library Supply Division, Denington Estate, Wellingborough, Northants NN8 2QT. Tel: 0933 224351. Send catalogues only.
- Dawson Book Division, Crane Close, Denington Road, Wellingborough, Northants NN8 2QG. Tel: 0933 274444.

- Greenhead Library Supply, Oldgate, Huddersfield HD1 6QH. Tel: 0484 644424.
- Heffers Booksellers, Orders Handling Department, Clifton House, Rustat Road, Cambridge CB1 4FY. Tel: 0223 358351. Send catalogues only.
- Macaulay Book Co, The Studio, Waverley Road, Rustington, West Sussex BN16 2DY. Tel: 0903 785966.
- Peters Library Service, 120 Bromsgrove Street, Birmingham B5 6RL. Tel: 021 666 6646. Specialise in children's books.

A valuable source of bookshops and specialist suppliers from which libraries purchase stock is the *List of Library Booksellers*, made up of the members of the Library Booksellers Group of the Booksellers Association. The Federation of Radical Booksellers should also be able to supply a list of their members active in this field.

Other Methods of Selling to Libraries

Some publishers sell to libraries – and indeed to bookshops and other customers – on standing order and subscription schemes. This may be particularly appropriate if the books you publish are part of a titled series which certain purchasers will require automatically on publication.

As a first step, ensure your series is listed in *Ulrich's International Periodicals Directory* (see Bibliography) and *The Librarians' Handbook* which is published annually by EBSCO Subscription Services (see Addresses). Both are used extensively by serial librarians and researchers worldwide.

If you develop a serious interest in serial publishing, you could join the UK Serials Group (see Addresses). They publish a journal called *Serials* and run various courses and conferences.

Standing Orders Begin by announcing the series and giving as much information about forthcoming and any backlist titles as possible. Prepare a leaflet or advert offering individual purchase of each volume or the chance to take out a standing order. Emphasise that this is an ideal way of avoiding the inconvenience of having to place a separate order every time you publish a title. A computerised database or even a simple card system will allow you to record each customer's requirements.

Customers will need to be invoiced when each title is sent, but be sure to quote the customer's reference or it will probably be returned. If the unit cost of each volume is low, to avoid the costs of processing several small payments some libraries may prefer to be billed every six months or even annually. If you are prepared to do this, say so in the publicity. Bookshops may occasionally want to return unsold copies of backlist volumes – this can of course cause problems so talk to your distributors and check their returns policy.

Subscriptions Subscriptions can be a little more difficult to administer, but if you are publishing volumes in a series frequently and regularly it may be worthwhile considering. Subscriptions usually run for twelve months. For a prepaid annual rate, which includes postage and usually represents a discount on the cost of each individual title, the subscriber will receive each volume as published throughout the year. As a publisher, the advantage is that you will at least be sure of a certain number of sales for each title in the series. It can lead to confusion and loss of good will, however, if your publishing programme is disrupted and you end up not publishing the proposed number of titles in the year. Be realistic and promise only what you can be sure to deliver. You must keep abreast of the consumer credit laws if you set up a subscription or standing order scheme.

According to recent estimates, up to 70 per cent of subscriptions to serials and journals are placed by libraries through subscription agents. Subscription agents provide a link between libraries and publishers by invoicing the library with one composite invoice and then placing orders with individual publishers for direct dispatch to the customer. This relieves the library of having to deal with lots of small accounts and can perhaps help minimise foreign exchange problems if ordering from overseas. As with bookshops, the subscription agent will require a discount on the annual rate, although it is much lower – usually around 5–10 per cent.

Many of the large international subscription agents, both in the UK and overseas, will write for details of your rates in the autumn for the subsequent year. If you are starting out it is a good idea to mail the main ones with your rates anyway; a list of the main agents (and booksellers who also act as subscription agents) is available from the British Council in their booklet *Ordering British Journals*. On your rate sheet, remember to include:

- the name of the series;
- the ISSN;
- the number of volumes expected;
- the frequency;
- any extra cost for airmail;
- the cost of backlist titles as well as the annual rate.

Incidentally, there is no reason why, as a book, each volume should not carry an ISBN as well as an ISSN. It is essential that each title also carries a sequential volume number or a similar code on the cover.

It is very important to maintain an up-to-date subscription or standing order list. Once it reaches a significant size, offering an exchange mailing with other like-minded publishers or charging others to include one of their flyers in each parcel can be a useful way of reaching a new audience or offsetting the costs.

Selling to Libraries Overseas

Tackling libraries outside the UK can be a more complicated business than selling to the domestic market. Many of the suppliers listed above sell overseas and the list *British Exporting Booksellers*, available from the British Council, will fill you in on their activities (see Bibliography). You will need to talk to your agents or distributors in each territory to make sure the market is well covered. They may be able to organise library mailings for you, suggest journals for review or put you in touch with specialist library suppliers in their territory.

It is perhaps worth paying particular attention to the vast library market in North America. If you have agents working for you in the USA and Canada, ensure that they mail copies of your books to the major library review journals such as *Choice* and *American Library Journal* which play a crucial role in the selection process. They should also ensure your books are displayed at the American Library Association regional and national fairs.

The continental European library market is increasingly attractive to British publishers and may well be worth exploring – Scandinavia and The Netherlands probably having the most potential. It is a difficult market to penetrate unless you have well established stock-holding distributors in the target countries, actively engaged in library supply. If, however, you are marketing to European libraries from the UK, one approach to consider is to rent a mailing list from a list broker (see Chapter 3). Specialists in this area include Alan Armstrong (see Addresses) who can provide lists of libraries and information centres throughout Europe (including the UK) and arrange mailings, exhibitions and a range of other dedicated services.

Marketing to the Educational Sector

Most books supplied to the school and college markets are produced by established educational publishers. These are highly competitive markets which you will find difficult to penetrate effectively without large resources. School material produced by educational publishers is aimed very much at the National Curriculum; likewise, college texts are geared towards established degree and diploma courses. In this book we can only hope to give a basic grounding in selling into this complex specialist market.

If you think your publication has school potential, or has been produced with this market in mind, test this by giving reading copies to a few teachers and asking for a realistic evaluation of the title's sales potential in schools. If their reply is encouraging, ask them for details of potential users, for example, age, attainment level, subject interest, type of school. This will allow you to gauge the size of the market and to whom to direct your promotion.

Likewise, if you find your book has potential in the college market, approach lecturers in the appropriate subject area for an opinion on its suitability. Will it have adoption possibilities? What is the competition?

Selling to Schools

Most schools buy the bulk of their textbooks from some 30 educational contractors around the country. In a few Local Education Authorities, such as Kent, Newcastle, Greater Manchester and Yorkshire, Direct Purchasing Organisations (DPOs) are responsible for the purchase of stocks for their schools.

Schools supplement their purchasing from these various sources by buying from booksellers. Figures suggest that school sales account for around 6 per cent of most bookshops sales (Publishers Association survey, 1988). Figures from the same survey also show that unit sales of school books in the UK declined by 29 per cent during the 1980s – from 46.9 million in 1981 to 33.6 million in 1988. Sales of consumer, university and professional books on the other hand all increased.

Most school textbooks and educational material (for example packs and videos) are placed outside the Net Book Agreement by their publishers, that is they are non-net books. The discounts offered to educational contractors is lower than for net books, usually 17.5 per cent.

A list of school suppliers is available from the Booksellers Association.

Promotion to Schools The standard promotion channels for most educational publishers are:

* direct mailing shots to teachers and advisers;
* exhibitions of education books;
* reviews and adverts in education magazines;
* reps visiting schools.

These methods of promotion are often supported by an inspection copy service. This allows teachers to obtain single copies on an adopt-purchase-or-return system so that they can examine the book in detail. This, however, can prove a very costly and time consuming service.

It costs upwards of £20,000 a year at commercial rates to keep a rep on the road, but if you have a few titles of interest to schools you may be able to come to an agreement with an educational publisher or an independent firm of school representatives who can show your titles to school teachers for a commission fee. Such arrangements are not always effective. Try asking around and seek a reference from a like minded organisation or company if you consider this worth pursuing.

If you work for a voluntary organisation with an established education programme, encourage staff liaising directly with schools to promote the material that supports your activities. This may prove to be the most effective way of getting your publications into the classroom.

Mailings to Schools Mailings to schools can be expensive – there are there are over 8,000 middle, secondary and special schools and around 25,000 primary schools both private and LEA run in the UK. Although it is of course far more effective to reach your target audience in a solus mailing (your material alone), on the grounds of cost you may have to opt for a shared mailing with another publisher producing similar books.

Perhaps the major problem in promoting to schools is reaching the right person at the right time. The right person in primary schools is usually the head teacher, in secondary schools the head of department. You may also decide to try school libraries. School secretaries will sometimes break up and distribute pieces of a mailing to appropriate people, if the pieces are marked.

Opinion varies on the best time to promote to schools. The most popular time for texts is January to March, with a peak in the second week of the January term. Less essential books will be ordered subsequently.

In your publicity material ensure you cover the basic information that teachers will need to know:

- sufficient detail about the contents and the theme;
- the reading age;
- how it relates to the requirements of the National Curriculum;
- the number of illustrations and pages and type of binding.

It can help to print a specimen double-page spread in your publicity material.

The tone of your copy for selling to teachers should be that of professional to professional. You should avoid the hard sell and sloganising but neither should you be bashful.

As well as teachers, ensure your mailings cover local authority subject advisers, HMIs (inspectors), teacher's centres and education lecturers. Addresses can be found in the *Education Yearbook* (Longman) or from the various mailing houses offering lists of addresses for mailing to the education sector. The main ones offering the largest lists are:

- Joynson Education Mailings;
- The Oxford Mailing Centre;
- The School Government Publishing Company (who also publish the *Education Authorities Yearbook*, a comprehensive source of secondary and tertiary educational establishments, LEAs and teacher's centres);
- Hamilton House.

Educational Book Stalls Stalls at general and specialised educational exhibitions can be useful. Details of exhibitions are available from the Exhibitions Organiser of the Educational Publishers Council (a division of the Publishers Association) and in educational papers, magazines and yearbooks. If you do participate in such events, remember that teachers visiting are far more likely to want to place orders or just take details rather than buy material on the spot. Take plenty of order forms, price lists and catalogues.

Resources and Reviews The more your publications are listed in teaching resource lists the better. Here, as elsewhere in the education field, teachers who are supporters of your work can help you by suggesting relevant lists.

You will also want to send review copies and press releases to the regular education periodicals.

The National Educational Resources Information Service (NERIS) provides on-line information on educational resources for teachers, lecturers and support agencies. For inclusion on their database library, send details of each title to NERIS (see Addresses).

Selling to Colleges

Unlike school texts, most books aimed at the college market are bought by individual students on the recommendation of lecturers responsible for planning courses.

Selected books will be put on reading lists usually classified as 'essential purchases' or as recommended background reading. Your task will be to bring your book to the attention of appropriate lecturers and, if it is selected, to ensure that the relevant college bookshop has an ample supply.

Promotion to Colleges Lecturers learn about titles suitable for their courses through a number of channels:

- reps visiting colleges to present new texts;
- direct mailings offering inspection copies;
- inserts and adverts in selected publications;
- word of mouth;

- reading reviews;
- picking up on new titles in bookshops and at exhibitions.

Unless your resources run to employing college travellers, your best bet is to concentrate on direct mail. Probably the most widely used list broker for the college market is IBIS (see Addresses) who supply wide-ranging national and international lists of academics and lecturers across the disciplines. For further details on list brokers see Chapter 3.

Lecturers will not expect elaborate brochures; a straightforward, factual leaflet detailing the essential points and offering the opportunity to request an inspection copy should suffice. Check out what the larger college publishers do and follow their example.

Ideally, publishers should produce an inspection copy questionnaire which will be sent out with the book. This will state how long the lecturer may keep the book before responding and indicate the procedures to be followed. It is normal practice for a lecturer to be allowed to keep an inspection copy gratis if they are recommending it to students as an essential purchase. Otherwise, they are obliged to return it or purchase it themselves within the stated period – usually 30 days.

The questionnaire should also ask for details of the course for which the book is required, the number of students on it, the starting date and the name of the local college bookshop.

If your title is only specific to a limited number of courses, rather than buying in lists that might include a large quantity of superfluous names try identifying suitable sample copy recipients and mail a gratis copy to each inviting comments – it may work out cheaper in the long run.

Back up this major promotional effort with review-copy mailings to periodicals in the field. Ask your author for recommendations and see Chapter 3.

Reprographic Copying The amount of reprographic copying that occurs in schools and colleges could considerably damage the sales of educational publishers. There are special problems in restricting photocopying in educational institutions and the Educational Publishers Council has sought ways of ensuring that a fair deal is given to publishers. Further details from the EPC and from the Copyright Licensing Agency (see Addresses).

8

Wholesale and Export

After taking up all the opportunities presented by selling directly to bookshops and library suppliers, you may wish to extend your market by considering making bulk sales to wholesalers and exploring the overseas market.

Wholesalers

Unless you are publishing titles likely to be of interest to a very wide range of general booksellers, it is unlikely that you will need the non-specialist wholesalers to handle your titles. Given that they are primarily interested in books with high unit sales from the major commercial houses, it is equally unlikely that they will have much enthusiasm for your titles. However, it is as well to be aware of the possibilities and range of wholesalers available.

Compared to many Western countries, the UK has a relatively small wholesaling industry but it has being growing rapidly over the last few years and shows no sign of slowing down. Approximately 30 per cent of paperbacks now pass through the hands of wholesalers and some 15 per cent of hardbacks (source: Euromonitor).

No two wholesalers are the same, but it is generally the case that they concentrate on supplying the fast selling titles from the larger publishers. Their reputations are usually made on the range of titles they handle and their speed of supply.

Smaller bookshops and shops selling books as only one component of their business tend to be the greatest users of wholesalers as they enable them to purchase a wide range of different publishers' titles from a single source. The downside of this for the bookseller is that wholesalers sometimes offer lower terms to their customers than the originating publisher's main distributor.

Like bookshops, wholesalers order stock from publishers' representatives or from seasonal catalogues. Due to the large volume of business they handle, they are able to negotiate better discounts and credit terms than most retailers and, in general, will be unwilling to consider titles offered at less than 50 per cent discount on 90 days credit. They will also expect you to accept returns of unsold copies. They will need to be convinced that your titles are likely to be in regular demand from a wide range of shops and it will be helpful if you can give them details of publicity planned to elicit demand.

Before approaching wholesalers, consider carefully whether or not they are likely to increase the sales of your titles dramatically. Remember that their discount requirements are greater than those of the retail trade and unless they are likely to shift your publications in volume, your margins will be reduced substantially.

In addition to the general wholesalers, there is also a range of specialist wholesalers catering to specific interest groups such as music and travel. As well as supplying the regular booktrade, they are particularly strong in the supply of books to outlets that sell books alongside a range of other goods and you should definitely bear them in mind if you are publishing in one of the subject areas for which they cater. These will be outlets that are unlikely to be covered by general trade representatives and they could make a considerable difference to your sales.

There are some 90 companies classified as wholesalers operating within the book trade in the UK and Ireland. Many of these are listed in the Booksellers Association *Directory of Book Publishers, Distributors and Wholesalers*. If you can't find what you want there, call one of your target outlets and find out which companies they use.

General Trade Wholesalers

Brief details of a range of trade wholesalers is given below. This list is by no means exhaustive and does not include wholesalers specialising in specific subject areas.

J Barnicoat This Cornish wholesaler is undergoing rapid expansion and seems likely to be a major force in the 1990s. Strong emphasis on paperback supply. Address: Parkengue, Kernick Road Industrial Estate, Penryn, Cornwall TR10 9EP. Tel: 0326 72628.

Bertram Books A Norwich based wholesaler with one of the largest range of both hardback and paperback titles available. Offer a nationwide service and have contacts with the majority of UK booksellers. Unlikely to consider titles much outside the mainstream. Address: The Nest, Rosary Road, Norwich NR1 1TF. Tel: 0603 663333.

Bookspeed Based in Edinburgh, Bookspeed are comparative newcomers having started their service in 1986. They supply green, women's and new age lists in addition to a wide range of general titles. Offer a nationwide service though are particularly strong in Scotland and the north of England. Address: 48A Hamilton Place, Edinburgh EH3 5AX. Tel: 031 225 4950.

Eason and Son Ltd Ireland's leading wholesaler. Also have a branch in Northern Ireland. Address: Brickfield Drive, Crumlin, Dublin 12, Ireland. Tel: 010 353 1 536211.

Gardners One of the larger firms handling hardbacks as well as paperbacks. Address: Providence Way, Eastwood Road, Bexhill-on-Sea TN39 3PT. Tel: 0424 224777.

Hammicks Part of the Hammicks bookselling chain but operated separately, the wholesale division supplies a wide range of titles to the general trade as well as to the group shops and John Menzies, their parent company. Address: Unit 18–20, Rosevale Road, Park House Industrial Estate, Newcastle-under-Lyme, Staffs ST5 7QT. Tel: 0782 5610000.

Heathcote Books Owned by W H Smith, Heathcote have a special relationship with the Waterstones/Sherratt & Hughes group which is also owned by WHS. However, their substantial operation is not confined to these shops and a nationwide service is provided. Address: Hawks Drive, Heathcote Estate, Warwick CV34 6LX. Tel: 0926 451555.

Pipeline Part of the Namara group which also owns Quartet Books and the Women's Press, Pipeline is probably the major wholesaler serving the London trade. Address: 32 Paul Street, London EC2. Tel: 071 729 3491.

Turnaround Specialise in distribution for small publishers but also run a small wholesale operation handling selected titles from more mainstream presses. Emphasis is on black interest, gay/lesbian issues and Irish politics and literature. Address: 27 Horsell Road, London N5 1XL. Tel: 071 609 7836/7.

Exporting

For many publishers, the export market will offer numerous opportunities for increasing the sales of their titles. In spite of increased competition from the US, the UK is the world's largest book exporter, with total export sales of books and related materials standing at £745.9 million in 1990. This figure represents about 27 per cent of total output and excludes royalties and other income derived from rights' sales and the publishing activities of overseas subsidiaries, which are worth at least another £350 million. If you are publishing books with overseas sales potential, this is a substantial market which it can prove foolish to ignore.

Perhaps the most important point to remember when entering the export market is that your target country's book trade may be very different to the domestic one. Wholesaling, for example, may be very much more prominent than in the UK; carriage charges may generally be paid by the bookseller rather than the publisher (as in the US); books may carry VAT or other duty; retail price maintenance is unlikely to apply and even if it does will probably not affect imports.

Export Markets
Table 8.1 shows the value of books exported from the UK in 1990 to some of the major overseas markets.

Table 8.1: Value of UK Book Exports in 1990

	£m
North America	129.8
Australia & New Zealand	88.0
The Netherlands	41.4
Irish Republic	36.3
Germany (West)	35.2
Japan	28.9
India	13.5

(Source: Euromonitor)

Obviously it is worth bearing in mind the size of these markets when you make your first foray into exporting. They have grown large because of the wide interest in English language books within them and may well be the most receptive to your products. It is interesting to note that The Netherlands, although relatively small in population terms, has a voracious appetite for British books which made up 18.5 per cent of total sales (£222.2 million) of British books into EC countries in 1990.

Note too that certain small export markets are much more significant for particular types of publishing than for the industry as a whole; the Middle East, for example, has traditionally been an important market for UK publishers issuing books for English language teaching.

Modes of Exporting
There are a number of options open to you if you want to sell your books into the export markets. These can be summarised as:

- Establishing distribution arrangements with a company based in the target area – known as a stock-holding agent.
- Marketing your books from the UK with the help of overseas repping agencies and wholesalers.

- Selling books through the UK's numerous exporting booksellers.
- Selling direct to the end-purchaser in the target markets.
- Selling rights to, or co-publishing with, a foreign publisher.

The permutations are many and varied and which methods suit your list will depend very much on your publishing programme. Remember though that the options are not necessarily mutually exclusive and a combination of several may best suit your needs.

The specialist field of selling rights and co-publishing is tackled in Chapter 9.

Overseas Distributors

If you are hoping to establish a presence in overseas markets, particularly outside of Europe, then your best method will probably be to appoint stock-holding distributors based in those markets. This way your books will be easily obtainable by the book trade who will be inclined to treat them in the same way as locally produced titles.

Ideally you will find arrangements that combine distribution with a full repping service to the trade outlets in each market. If such a service is not available, you may have to contract each separately (see the next section, Overseas Sales Agents).

If you are a new or small publisher, finding a good distributor willing to handle your titles may prove difficult, but do persevere. Check your competitors' catalogues to see who they use and ask around for recommendations. You can also approach publishers of a similar nature in the target market who might be willing to carry your list along with their own. Additionally, there are booksellers who will be prepared to operate as stock-holding agents if they have a strong interest in the type of books you are publishing. The major international book fairs are obvious venues to search out the possibilities.

Making agreements with overseas distributors requires you to be specific and detailed. Ensure that you establish a basis for mutual understanding at the start of your relationship; it can often be difficult and expensive to resolve problems which may arise. Your overseas distributor must not be treated as an afterthought and full consideration should be given to their requirements. Their needs may well be different to those in the domestic market.

When appointing a distributor, it is likely that you will be required to supply stock on a consignment basis similar to the arrangements you have made for the UK market. Details such as payment terms, however, are likely to differ from your domestic distribution arrangements.

You must establish whether the arrangement you have made is exclusive. For example, if you are setting up a distribution arrangement in Australia, your distributor may well ask that it be an exclusive arrangement which means that you may not sell your titles into that market via any other distributor or direct from the UK. You must consider very carefully whether this is wise. The distributor may feel that it is necessary if they are going to put a lot of work into selling and promoting your titles but if sales do not go well, you may be left without other options until your contract expires.

With overseas distribution you should be aware of the local legal requirements and documentation required for customs. These can be awkward and more binding than you might like. For details consult the volume *Hints to Exporters* for the country concerned (available from your local DTI office – see below).

You must establish in what currency payments will be calculated and on what price. In general, it is probably safest to ask for payment in sterling based on the UK retail price. Be clear on when you expect payments to be made and by what method. Direct transfer to your own bank may well prove safer and more convenient than cheques.

Discuss with your overseas distributors at the outset the best method of transporting the stock to them. They may well have an arrangement with a shipper or forwarder in the UK for bulk freight. If you need to make your own arrangements, your British distributor should be able to help or make recommendations and, if you are envisaging doing substantial overseas business, it is well worth checking out their expertise in this area before signing your initial contract. A useful source of shippers and forwarders is the annual London International Book Fair catalogue.

Bear in mind that should your overseas contract come to an end, or if you find you have supplied the distributor with too much stock, you may well be faced with shipping titles back to the UK at your own expense or abandoning them if this does not prove cost effective.

Overseas Sales Agents

Most small publishers will have difficulty in finding a stock-holding distributor outside of the US and Australia and, unless you are able to join together with a larger publisher, it is may be best to work with an agency on a commission basis.

The overseas agents listed in most publishers' catalogues are not always stock-holding distributors. Often they are agencies selling and promoting books to the trade which will be supplied and invoiced from the publisher's UK based distributor. You can usually find out more about them by writing off for information or by contacting the British publishers for whom they act. Some agencies work exclusively for one or two publishers but many work in much the same way as freelance representatives in the UK and are paid a percentage of net area sales, usually between 10 and 15 per cent.

If you decide to use an agency, they will need to be kept well informed of your publishing programme and up-to-date with a regular supply of AI sheets, covers, catalogues, etc. Remember that overseas markets can be very different from the UK and your agent's requirements may be different as well. Remember too that your books will be competing with those from your agency's other clients as well as those produced indigenously. Unless your books are particularly appropriate for the market in question, it may take some time to build up the good relationship with the agent necessary to achieve satisfactory results.

Not all agents covering the export market are based in the territory and you may find UK based agents who cover various export markets. Most of these cover Europe but others travel further afield, to the Middle East and Africa for example. In some cases, an agent may be prepared to consider just one or two of your titles if particularly appropriate to the market in which they specialise.

See below for information on fulfilling export orders.

Selling through British Booksellers

Many of the risks of exporting are avoided when your books go overseas through a British bookseller. Shops that do a considerable amount of export business are marked as such in the Booksellers Association *List of Members*. A list is also available in *British Exporting Booksellers* (British Council). Ensure you include the prominent ones in your mailings of advance information and catalogues and identify the ones specialising in areas of importance to you.

Selling Direct to the End Purchaser

Whether or not you are employing an overseas agent or distributor to handle your trade sales, there may still be openings to develop direct mail sales to libraries and individuals outside of the UK.

Your first task will be to identify those markets likely to have an interest in your titles. Once this is established, find out what address lists are available covering the target areas and direct your mailings accordingly (see also Chapter 3). To determine whether you will need to adapt your promotional leaflets, ask yourself:

- What methods of payment will you accept (e.g. credit card, giro, international money order, etc)?
- Should you be requesting postage at different rates for Europe and the rest of the world?
- Do you want to offer to supply by airmail as well as surface mail?
- In which currencies will you accept payment?
- Should prices be in another currency?
- Are you prepared to send goods without prepayment or will you issue a pro-forma invoice for payment prior to dispatch?
- Will giving a local address for orders encourage customers?

Export Trade Order Fulfilment
If you are receiving orders from overseas booksellers, either via your sales agents or unsolicited, your UK distributor should be able to process them, but it may be as well to check that they are familiar with the various customs formalities and documentation requirements. You should also be aware that credit periods will be longer for exports than for domestic sales and that your distributor may well want 120 days to pay you on these transactions rather than the more usual 90 days.

Whether you are using a distributor or not, it is as well to be aware of the formalities that exist between booksellers, shippers and publishers for the handling of export orders.

Unlike arrangements for the home market, carriage is normally charged on orders destined overseas. Some overseas booksellers, however, have shipping agents, or forwarders, in the UK and will ask that their orders be directed to them, free of carriage charges, for onward transportation. On bulk orders for substantial quantities of books, arrangements may be different and you may have to negotiate who should pay freight costs and insure the goods in transit. Two of the most common arrangements are known as Free on Board (FOB) and Cost, Insurance, Freight (CIF). FOB means that the seller's responsibility is limited to getting the books to a ship or aircraft and thereafter the responsibility is that of the purchaser. CIF means that the seller is responsible for freight, insurance and other costs to the purchaser's door. Unless discount arrangements suggest otherwise, it is better to try and arrange an FOB agreement if possible.

United States
The US accounts for some 20 per cent of the British publishers' export market and is likely to be one of the first to attract new publishers. As such it deserves special attention in your export efforts.

It is a market of big risks and high costs and should be approached with caution; you will need to study it carefully before venturing in if you are not to lose out on its potential. Some of the salient features are:

- its huge geographical size which means that many operations are regional;
- higher discounts given to bookshops;
- high levels of returns which vary enormously from title to title;
- large chains of discount booksellers;
- extensive promotion and selling by mail;
- a prominent stratum of wholesalers;
- heavy competition from local publishers;
- a vast library market.

Most UK publishers still hope to put their books into the US by selling rights to an American publisher. This allows for the British publisher to receive payment forward and gives the book local promotion and the best chance of large sales. Where this isn't possible, you may be able to find an American publisher willing to buy bulk copies of the British printing, possibly bearing the US publisher's imprint. This can extend the British printing and thus keep the unit cost of each book down.

Another method of entering the US market is through one of the distribution/sales companies. Such companies will provide an order fulfilment and cash collection service plus a certain amount of marketing through repping and catalogue mailings. If you can find one that works well for you this may even be more lucrative than selling rights. Some publishers claim that they would prefer to sell 1,000 'hard' copies, and retain an international profile, than sell 5,000 copies on a rights deal.

Terms for the provision of distribution services in the US will vary but it is unlikely that they will cost the publisher less than 55 per cent of the retail price of each book sold. Freight to the distributors and returns to the UK of unsold stock will usually be at the expense of the publisher but may be negotiable depending on discount arrangements. Services provided will also vary considerably and publishers are advised to look very carefully at contracts prior to reaching an agreement. In some cases you will need to appoint more than one distributor to ensure complete coverage of the territory. Companies currently offering a distribution and sales service in the USA for British publishers include: InBook, Book People, Consortium and the Talman Co (see Addresses).

Assistance with Exporting

There are several government agencies which can provide useful assistance with exporting.

British Council An important aspect of the British Council's work is the provision of British books and information about them to overseas countries. Their magazine *British Book News* is used extensively by overseas bookbuyers. In addition, the British Council maintain libraries in their overseas offices and send over 200 exhibitions of books overseas each year. The Council is represented in 87 countries where it runs 143 offices, 116 libraries and 53 English teaching centres. In London, they have an archive of information on book promotion in the export markets. Free booklets include *Sellers of British Books in The Netherlands, Sellers of British Books in Japan, British Publishers' Representatives in Japan* and *British Publishers' Representatives in India,* all available from the British Council Library, Books and Information Division (see Addresses). *Sellers of British Books in Germany* is available at £10 from the British Council, Library and Information Services, Hahnenstrasse 6, 5000 Cologne 1, Germany.

British Overseas Trade Board Another useful organisation is the British Overseas Trade Board. Among their services is the provision of information on overseas markets and on the documentation required when sending goods to these markets. They also fund export market research undertaken by British businesses and are a source of grants for attending meetings and fairs overseas. You can obtain details of these and their other services from your regional Department of Trade and Industry office. The DTI's *Export Publications Catalogue* listing more than 650 titles to help UK firms develop overseas markets may also provide a useful source of information. It is available free from DTI Export Publications (see Addresses).

Export Credits Guarantee Division One of the major worries in exporting is that of not being paid. Through a government department, the Export Credits Guarantee Division (see Addresses), it is possible to insure against this risk and other financial risks of exporting through their Export Finance Scheme. The ECGD also enable their clients to obtain access to cheaper export finance. To obtain ECGD cover you must contact them *before* you make an export deal, although once you become a policy holder this will not always be necessary.

Central Office of Information This is another government service of occasional use to exporting British publishers (see Addresses). Among other roles, the COI disseminates information abroad on British products, particularly if they will make a good news or feature item in foreign media which will be to Britain's credit.

You should be aware that these government related organisations may be unwilling to give assistance to you if the material you publish is seen as being critical of HMG or detrimental in some way to the 'nation's interests'.

If you are a member of the Publishers Association, you can make use of their export arm the Book Development Council which provides information and advice on practically all aspects of book exporting. Their monthly bulletin *Export News* is available to members only, but their reports on trade missions are available to all.

9

Rights, Book Clubs, Book Fairs and Prizes

Rights

The subjects of copyright and the buying and selling of rights are complex and a detailed consideration is beyond the scope of this book. However, it is important that even the smallest of publishers be conversant with the rudiments and we have therefore included a brief introduction to this topic. Those requiring a more thorough grounding should seek expert advice.

Copyright

As soon as you start publishing your own list of titles you will become involved in the area of copyright. This is the legal protection that gives authors and illustrators control over the ownership of their work. Ensure that you state who owns copyright on the work you have published on the verso of the title page, along with CIP data, accompanied by the formal copyright symbol: ©.

Control of copyright is one of the most valuable assets in publishing today and the value of many publishers is considerably enhanced by the rights they control through copyright licences. This is a specialised area of publishing and a good rights manager will spend a considerable amount of time keeping up to date with developments in copyright law, both nationally and internationally.

The international agreements on copyright law are governed by the Geneva Convention. Most countries are signatories to this protocol; be aware, though, that some countries are not and accordingly may not respect ownership.

If you have a serious interest in this aspect of publishing, and want to develop expertise as a rights manager, more information on the subject can be found by contacting the British Copyright Council (see Addresses) and the Copyright Licensing Agency (see the section on Reprographic Copying in Chapter 7).

The International Publishers Association (see Addresses), also publish information on copyright law.

Rights Contracts

Most standard contracts between publishers and authors contain clauses granting the publisher an exclusive right to publish and sell their work in a variety of editions, languages and markets. These clauses vary to a large extent depending on the nature of the publisher, the material being considered and the reputation of the author. They may cover all possible editions and markets or may be restricted to particular formats, territories and languages. They may also contain clauses giving the publisher an interest in any subsidiary rights which cover such areas as serial rights, film rights and broadcasting rights. A publisher may choose to exploit these rights or may licence other companies to do so. Much depends on what is in the contract.

Revenue received from selling or licensing rights is usually divided between author and publisher. How much each receives is open to negotiation, but standard publishing contracts usually split income 60/40 in favour of the author.

The Society of Authors and The Writers' Guild of Great Britain represent writers' interests in their dealings with publishers. Consult with them if you want to ensure that you are giving your authors a fair deal but beware that many of their recommendations are actually very difficult for small or new publishers of specialist books to comply with.

Selling Rights

Many publishers and authors use rights or literary agents to negotiate the sale and licensing of their work. Most of the prominent ones are listed in the *Writers' and Artists' Yearbook*. You probably will not need an agent for straightforward negotiations, but they are often seen as essential for complex deals and for selling into certain foreign language markets.

Start thinking about the potential for rights sales as early as possible in the life of your books and draw up a list. Depending on your titles, this could cover:

- foreign language rights;
- US rights;
- trade paperback rights;
- mass market paperback rights;
- book club rights;
- pre-publication serial rights;
- other subsidiary rights: eg film, radio, cassette.

Circulate information on your forthcoming titles to prospective publishers or agents, giving the essential details needed to enable them to assess the potential. For each title a photocopy of the copyright page, together with a table of contents, an AI sheet and, if you have it, a cover will be sufficient as a first move. A list of publishers in other parts of the world can be drawn up from a number of sources such as international book fair catalogues and directories of book publishers in the target countries. Follow up this with reading copies if requested.

Foreign Rights
If you sell foreign rights to a publisher, you are giving them the sole right to publish the title in the market in question, in the specified language(s) and edition(s). The two sections that follow look briefly at selling English language rights to US publishers and selling foreign language rights to publishers for translation.

US Rights The largest market for English language editions is the US and the licensing of your books to US publishers could be lucrative. Bringing your titles to the attention of US publishing houses can be done through the mail or through direct contact at one of the international book fairs, for example, Frankfurt. If a US publisher is interested in your books, you will need to negotiate a contract. This could either take the form of a joint printing of the US and UK editions or the production of a US edition by the US publisher.

The first option will involve you in selling finished copies or sheets at an agreed price. As with all legal transactions, you will need to examine the contract on offer or draw up your own. Whichever is the case, it is advisable to take expert advice and ensure that the agreement addresses the following:

- How will production costs be allocated?
- What method of shipping is required?
- How will shipping and insurance costs be allocated?
- What are the royalty arrangements?
- What type of paper should be used?
- What is the schedule of production?
- How many copies should be printed?
- How should they be bound?
- Are there penalty clauses, eg for late delivery?
- Will advance copies be required and, if so, how many?
- Will extra covers be required?
- What is the schedule of payments?

Once you have agreed the contract, it is most important that all clauses are closely adhered to as failure to comply can lead to disaster. Many US university presses, for instance, insist that their books should be printed on acid-free paper – a detail that one British publisher overlooked. They consequently found, to their horror, that the books were rejected as unacceptable and an entire printing had been wasted.

The second option open to publishers wishing to work with US counterparts is licensing the US publisher to produce their own edition for an agreed royalty. The standard form of royalty is 10 per cent of the net receipts and you should try to negotiate to be paid half the royalty on the first printing as an advance. Most publishers selling rights to US houses retain an exclusive right to sell their own edition in the traditional British Commonwealth market. However, the other world markets are often opened up to the US publisher who can then compete with the originating publisher for sales of the English language edition.

Foreign Language Rights If your books are likely to have wider international appeal, you can also consider selling translation rights which license other publishers to produce the work in a foreign language. Selected publishers should be approached and offered the option to take up rights on a particular title. A fixed period of time – usually three months – is allowed for them to reach a decision. If your title is accepted, the foreign language publisher should pay a small advance on signing the agreement and, within a specified period of time, will produce their own edition. Royalties on net sales will then be paid against sales made. Alternatively, a flat fee may be considered. Royalty levels and advances on foreign language editions in the normal course of events tend to be lower than those obtainable for US rights.

Other Rights

Paperback Rights If you have published your titles in hardback, you may decide to publish a paperback edition yourself or sell rights for a paper edition to a larger publisher. Occasionally you may even find yourself in a position to sell rights to one of the more commercial paperback houses even if the original edition was published in paper.

If this option appeals to you, try to find out which companies would be interested in re-issuing your titles or buying paperback rights. It could enable you to reach a wider audience and perhaps help finance future projects.

If you make a deal with a larger commercial publisher, make sure that you get your due. Too often small publishers are so pleased to see a large house taking up their product that they fail to ensure that they and their authors benefit sufficiently. A literary agent can conduct negotiations on your behalf if necessary. Even if the original edition was published in paper, you may be able to negotiate a deal allowing you to continue to sell your edition as a 'trade' paperback, leaving the 'mass-market' edition to the new publisher.

Some non-commercial publishers reject the approaches of commercial publishers out of hand. If you are thinking of doing this, remember that the commercial publisher may then engage your author direct or commission a similar work from another source. A workable compromise may be to reach an agreement whereby the re-issue carries your imprint alongside that of the new publisher.

Book Club Rights If the opportunity arises, you may also want to consider selling book club rights. For more information on negotiating with book clubs, see the section on Book Clubs below.

Serial Rights These are more accurately known as first (or pre-publication) serial rights and second (after publication) serial rights. Provided that you, and not the author, control them, they are rights you can sell to a newspaper or magazine to enable them to serialise or extract large parts of your title, usually on an exclusive basis.

It is difficult to generalise about the potential income that can be produced from selling serial rights. Much depends on the interest in the title. Revenue from first serial rights can be as low as £100 for a book of local interest in a particular area or up to £100,000 for a sale to a major national newspaper. Second serial rights are far less lucrative.

It should be pointed out that it is very rare for small publishers to pull off such deals. There is no point in wasting time approaching the press if there is no realistic likelihood of a sale. On the other hand, you may decide to allow a sympathetic magazine to publish an extract from your book for free, both to spread your message and to promote sales of your publication.

Useful books on the subject of rights include: *Selling Rights: A Publisher's Guide to Success* by Lynette Owen, *Handbook of Copyright in British Publishing Practice* by Jean Cavendish and *Publishing Agreements: A Book of Precedents* by Charles Clark (see Bibliography).

Book Clubs

About 2,000,000 people in the UK are members of book clubs (source: Euromonitor), the majority of these being in socio-economic groups A and B. They belong to clubs licensed by the Publishers Association which are allowed to sell books at less than the full published price.

There are approximately 50 book clubs in operation in the UK, although over half of these are part of Book Club Associates (owned by Reed International and Bertelsmann) and Readers Union (owned by David & Charles), which probably account for over 50 per cent of all members in the UK. All book clubs used to be reprint clubs and many still are. They are permitted to sell their editions nine months after the publication of the original edition. However, in 1968 the Publishers Association started to license simultaneous book clubs which issue their choices at approximately the same time as trade editions are published.

The major clubs are listed in the *Writers' and Artists' Yearbook* and flaunt their interests in the Sunday newspaper colour supplements and other magazines. The Publishers Association should be able to provide you with a complete list. You may find that there are also specialist book clubs operating in your field of interest. Book clubs sell to their subscribing members. They usually build up a membership by advertising and distributing leaflets to likely segments of the public, their promotion activities being targeted to the general public or to the specialist interest groups at which many of their titles are directed. On joining, members agree to purchase a minimum number of books from the club each year at a price set lower than the retail price at which these titles sell in bookshops.

Selling to Book Clubs

Prospective book clubs need to be contacted as early as possible in the publishing process as they will probably want to see proofs of your titles for consideration.

Large book clubs are hard bargainers so you are unlikely to get much of a contribution to overheads from them. They will probably buy at 20–25 per cent of your retail price. Although the profit margin is therefore tiny, if you add their printing on to your own, the economies of scale can substantially bring down your unit cost – and remember sales are all firm. If you are selling to a small book club, they are more likely to simply take your standard edition and ask for a discount off the list price of around 50 per cent. Probably the major financial advantage is the improvement rendered to your cash flow by a sale to a book club which brings in money early in the life of a book.

As regards impact, communication and readership, the advantages are more palpable. You make your title available to many people who are beyond easy reach of a bookshop and to others who either do not use bookshops or who enjoy the pre-selection offered by a book club. It may well be that non-members will also see the club's advertising and be persuaded to buy the book from a shop at the full price.

Book Fairs

Book fairs present valuable opportunities to meet other publishers, sell and acquire rights, meet customers, agents and distributors and generally find out what is going on in the publishing world. However, they can be expensive, time consuming and exhausting and attendance should be treated with caution. It can be very disappointing to spend a lot of time and energy at a fair only to come away feeling you have achieved nothing.

Select which fairs you need to attend with care and plan your itinerary and appointments in advance. Decide whether or not you need to book a stand to exhibit your titles or whether you could just as well manage by visiting the stands of the people you need to see.

Most fairs are written up in *The Bookseller* and one good way of finding out about them is by reading the previous year's report. It also publishes a list of international fairs being held throughout the year. Brief details of some of the more interesting events follow:

Overseas Fairs

Frankfurt Book Fair The most famous and largest of all book fairs is held each year in Frankfurt at the beginning of October. It is an enormous event attended by publishers from all over the world. Most of the business is rights sales between publisher and publisher or packager. It can also be a useful venue to meet overseas booksellers and agents.

It is possible to attend the fair as a visitor, but if you decide that you need to book a stand, this can be arranged through the fair's offices (see Addresses). Demand is high and you will need to book at least six months in advance, if not earlier. Although stand prices are not particularly cheap, the cost of a single unit is not prohibitive and it will give you a base and contact point. It is also possible to arrange a collective stand with other publishers and share the costs. The Independent Publishers Guild (see Addresses) also arrange joint stands for their members at Frankfurt and a number of other fairs.

Reasonably priced accommodation can be arranged through the fair's Frankfurt office when you arrive or during the week prior to the start. It is a mistake to think that you will be able to find a room under your own steam when you arrive – most hotels will have been booked up the previous year.

If you want to visit for a day or two, special charter flights are available which are advertised in *The Bookseller*.

Start planning your visit in August or before. Write to publishers and agents you hope to meet there and start fixing up a diary of appointments. Go armed with dummy books, catalogues and all the information you may need to transact your business. For a first-time visitor, the fair can be overwhelming and it is essential to be well prepared. Each year the publishers of the *Rough Guides* series produce a useful guide to Frankfurt for visitors to the Book Fair. Copies are available free from their stand at the fair, or write to them before you go: Rough Guides, 1 Mercer Street, London WC2H 9QL.

American Booksellers Association Convention Commonly referred to simply as 'ABA', this is the major US book fair, held at the very beginning of June in a different city each year. Although once thought of in the UK trade as an American version of Frankfurt, it is now being increasingly attended by British publishers large and small. If you are planning a visit, it is wise to register before mid-April.

Attending ABA can give you a good insight into what is going on in North American publishing and bookselling. As well as large displays by publishers and distributors, the Convention runs numerous lectures and discussion groups for visitors which cover a wide variety of pertinent topics.

If you visit ABA, it is less likely that you will want a stand than at Frankfurt but a visit should give you plenty of opportunities to seek out new titles, sell rights or make distribution arrangements.

For further information, contact the American Booksellers Association (see Addresses).

Bologna Book Fair This fair is held annually in March and is devoted exclusively to children's books. Most children's book publishers attend, again to trade in rights and sell to overseas markets.

For further information, contact the Bologna Book Fair (see Addresses).

International Feminist Book Fair Perhaps the most truly international fair, the biennial IFBF has been held in major cities around the world since 1984. Venues to date include London, Barcelona, Oslo and Montreal. The fair is traditionally held towards the end of June and exhibitors should contact the organisers several months in advance.

For further information, contact the IFBF (see Addresses).

Also worth knowing about, but perhaps not worth a visit for the small publisher, are the fairs in Cairo, Jerusalem, New Delhi, Tokyo and Warsaw. Your local agent may well be in a position to cover these and others for you if appropriate.

Help with visiting overseas fairs is available from the Fairs & Promotion Branch, Department of Trade and Industry and by taking advantage of the subsidies offered by the British Overseas Trade Board through the offices of the Book Development Council of the Publishers Association (see Addresses).

UK Fairs

London International Book Fair This is the largest of the UK fairs and catered originally for small and specialist publishers. Over the last few years it has undergone rapid expansion and now caters for the whole trade.

The LIBF is held annually in the spring at Olympia. Although occasionally shunned by some of the major houses who prefer to concentrate their energies on Frankfurt, it is now generally recognised as a major international fair. Like most other fairs, it is used by publishers to trade amongst themselves and also by booksellers and librarians who want to get an overview of what is available. Taking a stand can be expensive and, as opinions on its value vary, it's probably best to talk to publishers in the same line before making a booking.

For further information, contact LIBF (see Addresses).

Booksellers Association Conference Also of interest is the book fair attached to the annual Booksellers Association Conference which is held at a different location each year. Historically, it does not seem a very bright event although some publishers clearly put more into it than others. As with all of these fairs, it might be worth joining up with other publishers in similar fields if you decide to exhibit. This could help cut down on time and costs and could make an otherwise expensive event cost-effective.

Contact the BA for further details.

International Fair of Radical, Black and Third World Books This specialist book fair is held every two years each March in London. Attracting visitors from the Americas, the Caribbean and Africa, it is a major event in the calendar if you have books aimed at this interest group. It is one of the few fairs at which the public are actively encouraged to buy books.

The fair is open to teachers and members of the public as well as the trade. A series of lectures, performances and other cultural events is run alongside each fair giving it additional interest. Similar, though much smaller, fairs are organised in Bradford and Manchester around the same time.

For further information, contact the organisers (see Addresses).

London Irish Book Fair Another annual event is the London Irish Book Fair which is organised by Green Ink Bookshop. Here too the public are welcome and are encouraged to buy books. Certainly worth attending if your list includes books of Irish interest.

For further information, contact the organisers (see Addresses).

Small Press Group Annual Book Fair The SPG runs this lively fair for their members each September in London. They can also provide information on other small press fairs both in the UK and internationally. For further information, contact the SPG (see Addresses).

Prizes, Awards and Grants

Prizes and Awards

Many publications receive an added sales impetus if they are awarded one of the numerous prizes or awards on offer to writers. These range from the highly prestigious Booker Prize – worth £20,000 – to the Isaac Deutscher Memorial Prize – worth £100 – which is awarded in recognition of outstanding writing and research in the Marxist tradition of

Isaac Deutscher. Most of the big prizes are scooped by the major houses but the smaller ones should not be ignored and can bring recognition to your authors and imprint in general.

If you decide to enter a title for an award, always make sure that you discuss the matter first with the author. Not only is this courteous but it is possible your author may not want the book put forward for consideration.

If you do win an award, use it to promote your list wherever possible. If you are reprinting a winning or shortlisted title, say so on the front and back cover and tell your reps to bring it to the attention of booksellers. If a reprint is not imminent, a sticker on the front cover can also put the message across.

A list of prizes available can be obtained from the Book Trust who publish *A Guide to Literary Prizes, Grants and Awards*. Most of the major ones are also listed in the *Writers' and Artists' Yearbook* (A & C Black). Both publications give details of the criteria for the awards and where to apply.

Brief details of a selection of awards follow:

J R Ackerley Prize for Autobiography Given annually for works of literary autobiography. PEN, 7 Dilke Street, London SW3 4JE. Tel: 071 352 6303.

The Hans Christian Andersen Medals Awarded every two years to authors and illustrators of children's books. International Board on Books for Young People, Book Trust, Book House, 45 East Hill, London SW18 2QZ. Tel: 081 870 9055.

Arts Council Raymond Williams Memorial Award Awarded annually for books from community-based publishers. Arts Council of Great Britain, Literature Dept., 14 Great Peter Street, London SW1P 3NQ. Tel: 071 333 0100.

Arvon Foundation International Poetry Competition Awarded biennially for previously unpublished poems. Arvon Foundation Poetry Competition, Kilnhurst, Kilnhurst Road, Todmorden, Lancashire OL14 6AX. Tel: 0706 816582.

The Booker Prize Major annual prize (currently £20,000) awarded for fiction. Publicity Officer, Book Trust, Book House, 45 East Hill, London SW18 2QZ. Tel: 081 870 9055.

The Isaac Deutscher Memorial Prize c/o Gerhard Wilke, 75 St Gabriels Road, London NW2 4DU. Tel: 081 450 0469.

Fawcett Book Prize Annual award of £500 given to the book which does most to illuminate women's position in society. General Secretary, The Fawcett Society, 46 Harleyford Road, London SE11 5AY. Tel: 071 587 1287.

The Martin Luther King Memorial Prize Awarded to a literary work reflecting the ideals of Martin Luther King. John Brunner, c/o NatWest Bank, 7 Fore Street, Chard, Somerset, TA20 1PJ. SAE must be sent.

MIND Book of the Year – the Allen Lane Award Given to the author of any book which outstandingly furthers public understanding of mental health problems. MIND, 22 Harley Street, London W1N 2ED. Tel: 071 637 0741.

Scottish Arts Council Awards Various prizes made each year by the SAC to published books of literary merit written by Scots or writers resident in Scotland. Literature Dept., The Scottish Arts Council, 12 Manor Place, Edinburgh EH3 7DD. Tel: 031 226 6051.

Smarties Prize Three prizes for books for children of primary school age. Book Trust, Book House, 45 East Hill, London SW18 2QZ. Tel: 081 870 9055.

Whitbread Literary Awards Awarded to the best book in each of five categories: novel, first novel, children's novel, biography/autobiography and poetry. One is selected as Whitbread Book of the Year. Booksellers Association, 272–274 Vauxhall Bridge Road, London SW1V 1BA. Tel: 071 730 8214.

Finally, a mention should also be made of the *Sunday Times* Small Publishers Competition held annually and open to independent publishers producing between five and 40 titles each year. Details are available from Book Trust (see Addresses).

Grants
Most grants available to publishers in the UK are awarded to companies and organisations for the production of works considered to be of literary or artistic merit but of limited commercial appeal. Poetry, works in translation, oral histories, photography and minority interest projects are some of the more obvious areas. However, marketing is increasingly seen by funding bodies as an important and essential component of the publishing process and if you are applying for production awards, you will need to convince grant givers that your marketing plans are well formulated.

Such is the importance now given to marketing that some money may be available for developing marketing activities separate to specific publication awards. Much will depend, however, on the policies of the body you approach and the competition from other applicants.

Most of the grants on offer are made by the Arts Council of Great Britain (see Addresses) and the Regional Arts Boards. Address details and scope of funds available from them and other grant making bodies can be found in *The Arts Funding Guide* by Anne-Marie Dalton (see Bibliography).

10

Postscript: Evaluating your Marketing

Evaluation of Selling

How you evaluate your selling will depend on the objects of your publishing. Commercial houses tend to rely on the standard tool kit of turnover, return on capital invested, stockturn and profit. They will also evaluate the foundations they are laying for the future – their power to attract and develop authors, their reputation in the trade. Standard books on business explain this in detail.

One issue such books do not discuss is the rates of sale to bookshops that can be expected. If you have planned, you will have decided how many copies you hope to sell over a specified period. Rates of sale vary enormously from one style of publishing to another and from one title to another. For instance, large mass market paperback publishers reckon to sell much of their first print run before publication day. A newish small publisher is doing well to have sold 30 per cent of its first print run three months after publication day.

Evaluation of Promotion

Evaluating the effectiveness of promotions provides useful information for planning future campaigns.

If you are using direct selling methods, evaluating results need not be difficult. Using the response code on leaflets and adverts will allow you to identify most of the orders that result from the promotion (see Chapter 3).

If you are sending out order forms, these can be coded either by the printer or, more cheaply, by yourself. You can either draw lines down the edge of each batch in a specific position or in a specific colour or you can drill holes through each batch in a different position.

When counting the orders that result from a specific promotion, remember that many customers will not use the order form or clip-off coupon. To compensate for this, some publishers increase their recorded response by as much as 40 per cent to determine the 'real' response.

Evaluating sales from other types of publicity is more problematic, particularly so if the majority of your sales are going through the trade. If, for example, a title is reviewed or receives editorial coverage in the media you might rightly expect an increase in interest. However, unless orders are sent direct to you, it will be difficult to pinpoint exactly what stimulated demand.

If you are publishing in a particular subject area on a regular basis, then over a period of time you should be able to identify which of your promotion methods produces the best results. Try to identify these and bear them in mind when drawing up marketing plans for future publications.

Appendix 1

Publishing Check List

This check list is designed to remind a small publisher of the major steps in publishing and their sequence. Some titles will not require every step but it is as well to consider each step for each title to avoid missing out the essential stages.

In the smallest publishing operations, many of the functions which have been differentiated on this list will be the job of one person – the only person. This should not daunt you. After all, you do not have the problems of coordination and liaison that larger organisations suffer.

Preliminary Considerations

- What do we want to say? To whom? With what effect?
- Can we do this by publishing? Would another medium be more effective?
- Draw up a readership spectrum.
- How can we reach our intended readers? Through what promotion and marketing channels?
- Roughly how much will it cost? Can we afford this?
- Who could best write the publication?
- How can it be effectively distributed?
- Estimate the initial print run.
- Choose a working title.
- Evaluate the possibility of subsidiary and rights sales.

Commissioning and Planning Production

- Prepare a brief, commission authors, settle payment terms and dates, sign contract.
- Discuss format and presentation of MS (typescript, disk, etc).
- Obtain information about the author that might be useful for promotion.
- Keep in touch with the author. Provide help and encouragement.
- Chase author for MS; acknowledge receipt of MS.
- Pay author if an advance is due.
- Check MS for content and communication. Initiate editorial work required to prepare MS for typesetting.

102

- Ensure any copyright material has been cleared for reproduction.
- Choose the format.
- Decide on quantity of illustrations, if any. Line or tone?
- Unless any major revision is required, determine extent. Include in your calculations any index, prelims and supplementary material.
- Decide on style of binding (perfect bound, cased, other).
- Commission text designers and photographer or picture researcher.
- Set the cover design parameters (number of colours, weight of board, line or tone). Commission cover designer.
- Prepare specification from above.
- Commission foreword writer.
- Call for quotes from printers and typesetters.
- Complete editorial work and mark up for selected typesetter.
- Send for typesetting.
- Draw up the first promotion plan and cost it.
- Determine approximate list price.
- If changes are made to your plan, remember to adjust costing and pricing.
- Finalise the publishing schedule and set publication date.

Six Months Before Publication

- Draw up a more detailed promotion plan with help of distributor and author. Finalise budget.
- Write copy for front and back cover. Clear this with author. Decide on final title.
- Chase designer for cover.
- Chase designer or photographer for illustrations.

Three Months Before Publication

- Allocate ISBN and submit bibliographic forms to Whitaker.
- Prepare index and title, copyright and contents pages for type-setting.
- Prepare Advance Information sheet and mail to agents, representatives, library suppliers, authors, etc.
- Re-check pricing.
- Print covers, including advance covers.
- Send out advance covers to representatives, agents, library suppliers and others.
- Check that representatives have all the information they require for subscribing. Are any early arrangements required for launch?
- Author and editor proofread copies of the typesetting.

- Editor collates corrections and returns to typesetter.
- Editor checks corrections.

Two Months Before Publication

- Check rate of subscribing and finalise print run.
- Editor passes the order to print and obtains confirmation of delivery date.
- Write, design and print any publicity material such as a leaflet.
- Finalise promotion plan, schedule it and decide how to evaluate the various aspects.
- Prepare press and review list.
- Write press release and prepare review slips.
- Drum up media interest.
- Arrange any leaflet mailings or advertising.
- Send details of any expected media coverage to representatives.

Final Run-up to Publication

- Finished copies of book arrive.
- Send out authors' copies, review copies, copies for representatives and copyright deposit copies.
- Check advance orders with distributors and arrange delivery.
- Book author's time for media appearances. Chase press by phone as appropriate.
- Engage a press cutting agency if necessary.

Publication

- Attend launch!

Post Publication

- Continue promotion and keep track of rate of sale.
- Calculate actual cost and degree of error in estimate.
- Ensure any material required for a revised edition or reprint is stored.
- Keep a reprint copy in which you mark all errors.
- Some time later, evaluate the publishing of the title and particularly the promotion. Remember that it is the effectiveness of the promotion rather than the mere quantity of coverage that you wish to judge.

Appendix 2

Addresses

This is essentially a list of addresses relevant to this book. Further sources of addresses can be found in the various booktrade directories available (see Bibliography). The inclusion of a name in this list does not in any way constitute a recommendation.

Trade Contacts

- Anderson Rand, The Scotts Bindery, Russell Court, Cambridge CB2 1HL.
- Association of Little Presses, 89a Petherton Road, London N5 2QT. Tel: 071 226 2657.
  Membership available. Also publish 'how to' guides for the small publisher.
- Association of Subscription Agents, Periodicals Division, 410 Beaver House, Hythe Bridge Street, Oxford OX1 2SN. Tel: 0865 792792 x 212/213.
- Book Data Ltd, Northumberland House, 2 King Street, Twickenham, Middlesex TW1 3RZ. Tel: 081 892 2272. Fax: 081 892 9109.
- Book Industry Communications, 39–41 North Road, London N7 9DP. Tel: 071 607 0021.
  BIC works to carry out vital development work on trade systems and standards.
- Book Marketing Ltd, 15 Irving Street, London WC2H 7AU. Tel: 071 839 8845. Fax: 071 930 3424.
- Book Publishers' Representatives Association, 3 Carolina Way, Tiptree, Essex CO5 0DW. Tel: 0621 816710.
- Book Trust, Book House, 45 East Hill, London SW18 2QZ. Tel: 081 870 9055. Fax: 081 874 4790.
- Book Trust Scotland, 15a Lynedoch Street, Glasgow G3 6EF. Tel: 041 332 0391. Fax: 041 331 2645.
- Booksellers Association of Great Britain and Ireland, 272–274 Vauxhall Bridge Road, London SW1V 1BA. Tel: 071 834 5477. Fax: 071 834 8812.
- BOD: Order Distribution, 49 Victoria Road, Aldershot, Hants GU11 1SJ. Tel: 0252 20697.
- R R Bowker and Co, 245 W 17th Street, New York, NY 10011, USA.

- British Library National Bibliographic Services, Boston Spa, Wetherby, West Yorks LS23 7BQ. Tel: 0937 546612.
- Children's Book Foundation, Book House, 45 East Hill, London SW18 2QZ. Tel: 081 874 2718. Fax: 081 874 4790.
- Copyright Deposit – see British Library address above.
- Cyngor Llyfrau Cymraeg/Welsh Books Council, Castell Brychan, Aberystwyth, Dyfed SY23 2JB. Tel: 0970 624151.
- Educational Publishers Council, 19 Bedford Square, London WC1B 3HJ. Tel: 071 580 6321. Fax: 071 636 5375.
- Federation of Radical Booksellers, c/o Lifespan, Townhead, Dunford Bridge, Sheffield, S30 6TG.
- Feminist Book Fortnight, c/o Carole Spedding, 7 Loddon House, Church Street, London NW8 8PX. Tel: 071 402 8159. Fax: 071 402 1182.
- Independent Publishers Guild, 25 Cambridge Road, Hampton, Middlesex TW12 2JL. Tel: 081 979 0250.

  Founded in 1962 to offer a forum for the exchange of ideas and information in the changing world of publishing. Membership available. Holds regular meetings.
- International Publishers Association, 3 avenue de Miremont, 1206 Geneva, Switzerland. Tel: 010 41 22 46 30 18. Fax: 010 41 22 47 57 17.

  A non-governmental organisation of 45 national publishers' associations that aims to ensure the publisher's right to publish without hindrance. The IPA also works to ensure copyright protection and publishes information on copyright law.
- Irish Book Publishers Association, Book House Ireland, 65 Middle Abbey Street, Dublin 1, Ireland. Tel: 010 353 1 730108. Fax: 010 353 1 730620.

  Membership available.
- Library Association, 7 Ridgmount Street, London WC1E 7AE. Tel: 071 636 7543.
- Orders Clearing, c/o IBIS Information Services Ltd, Waterside, Lowbell Lane, London Colney, St Albans, Herts AL2 1DX. Tel: 0727 25209. Fax: 0727 26461.
- Publishers Association, 19 Bedford Square, London WC1B 3HJ. Tel: 071 580 6321/5. Fax: 071 636 5375.

  Membership available.
- Publishers Publicity Circle, 48 Crabtree Lane, London SW6 6LW. Tel: 071 385 3708.
- Radical Bookseller, 265 Seven Sisters Road, London N4 2DE. Tel: 081 802 8773.
- Scottish Publishers Association, The Scottish Book Centre, 137 Dundee Street, Edinburgh EH11 1BG. Tel: 031 228 6866. Fax: 031 228 4333.

- Small Press Group, BM Bozo, London WC1M 3XX. Tel: 0234 211606.
    Membership available.
- Standard Book Numbering Agency Ltd, 12 Dyott Street, London WC1A 1DF. Tel: 071 836 8911. Fax: 071 836 4342.
- Teleordering Ltd, 3 The Windmills, Turk Street, Alton, Hants GU34 1EF. Tel: 0420 544177. Fax: 0420 543930.
- Welsh Books Council – see Cyngor Llyfrau Cymraeg above.
- J Whitaker and Sons Ltd, 12 Dyott Street, London WC1A 1DF. Tel: 071 836 8911. Fax: 071 836 2909.
    Publish a range of publications for, by and about the UK book trade.
- Women in Publishing, 12 Dyott Street, London WC1A 1DF. Tel: 071 836 8911. Fax: 071 836 2909.

Distributors, Representatives and Sales Agents

A selection of those in the UK and the US willing to consider handling small publishers.

- Airlift Book Company, 26/28 Eden Grove, London N7 8EF. Tel: 071 607 5792. Fax: 071 607 6714.
    Sales, marketing and distribution.
- Biblios Publishers Distribution Services, Star Road, Partridge Green, West Sussex RH13 8LD. Tel: 0403 710971. Fax: 0403 711143.
    Distribution.
- Book People, 2919 5th Street, Berkeley, CA 94710, USA.
    Sales and distribution.
- Central Books, 99 Wallis Road, London E9 5LN. Tel: 081 986 4854. Fax: 081 533 5821.
    Sales and distribution.
- Consortium, 287 East 6th Street, Suite 365, St Paul, MN 55101, USA.
    Sales and distribution.
- Gazelle Book Services, Falcon House, Queen Square, Lancaster LA1 1RN. Tel: 0524 68765. Fax: 0524 63232.
    Sales and distribution.
- InBook, Box 120470, East Haven, CT 06512, USA.
    Sales and distribution.
- Password, 23 New Mount Street, Manchester M4 4DE. Tel: 061 953 4009. Fax: 061 953 4001.
    Sales and distribution (poetry only).
- Paul and Co, PO Box 442, Concord, MA 01742, USA.
    Sales, marketing and distribution.
- Talman Co, 150 5th Avenue, New York, NY 10011, USA.
    Sales, marketing and distribution.

- Turnaround Distribution, 27 Horsell Road, London N5 1XL. Tel: 071 609 7836/7. Fax: 071 700 1205.
  Sales, marketing and distribution.

Book Fairs

- American Booksellers Association Convention, 137 West 25th Street, New York, NY 10001, USA. Tel: 0101 212 463 8450. Fax: 0101 212 463 9353.
- Bologna Book Fair, Piazza Costituzione 6, 40128 Bologna, Italy. Tel: 010 39 51 282111. Fax: 010 39 51 282332.
- Department of Trade and Industry, Fairs & Promotion Branch, Dean Bradley House, 52 Horseferry Road, London SW1P 2AG. Tel: 071 276 2414.
- Frankfurt Book Fair, Reineckstrasse 3, D6000 Frankfurt am Main 1, Germany. Tel: 010 49 69 2102221. Fax: 010 49 69 2102227.
- International Fair of Radical, Black & Third World Books, 76 Stroud Green Road, London N4 3EN. Tel: 071 272 4889.
- International Feminist Book Fair, 7 Loddon House, Church Street, London NW8 8PX. Tel: 071 402 8159. Fax: 071 402 1182.
- London International Book Fair, Reed Exhibition Companies, Oriel House, 26 The Quadrant, Richmond upon Thames, Surrey TW9 1DL. Tel: 081 940 6065. Fax: 081 940 2171.
- London Irish Book Fair, 5 Archway Mall, The Archway, London N19 5RG. Tel: 071 263 4748.

Mailing Services and List Brokers

- A Mail, 23 New High Street, Headington, Oxford OX3 7AJ. Tel: 0865 741261. Fax: 0865 742024.
- Alan Armstrong, Hambleden, Henley-on-Thames, Oxon RG9 6SD. Tel: 0491 577767.
  Library specialist.
- British List Brokers Association, 16 The Pines, Broad Street, Guildford GU3 3BH. Tel: 0483 301311.
- Data Protection Registrar, Springfield House, Water Lane, Wilmslow, Cheshire SK9 5AX. Tel: 0625 535777.
- Hamilton House, 17 Staveley Way, Brixworth Industrial Park, Northampton NN6 9EL. Tel: 0604 881889. Fax: 0604 880735.
- IBIS Information Services Ltd, Waterside, Lowbell Lane, London Colney, St Albans, Herts AL2 1DX. Tel: 0727 25209.
- Joynson Education Mailings, PO Box 6, Abingdon, Oxon OX13 6EL. Tel: 0865 736361. Fax: 0865 326244.
- The Oxford Mailing Centre, PO Box 67, Oxford OX1 5JY. Tel: 0865 730030. Fax: 0865 730035.

- School Government Publishing Company, Darby House, Bletchingley Road, Merstham, Redhill RH1 3DN. Tel: 0737 642223.

Media Services

- BBC Local Radio, Programme Services Unit, The Langham, Portland Place, London W1. Tel: 071 977 4272.
- BBC World Service, Bush House, Strand, London WC2B 4BH. Tel: 071 240 3456.
- BRAD, 1a Chalk Lane, London NE4 0BU. Tel: 081 441 6644.
- Independent Radio News, Crown House, 72 Hammersmith Road, London W14 8YE. Tel: 071 333 0011.
- The Press Association, 85 Fleet Street, London EC4P 4AS. Tel: 071 353 7440. Fax: 071 936 2363.
- Reuters, 85 Fleet Street, London EC4P 4AS. Tel: 071 250 1122. Fax: 071 583 3769.
- Tellex Monitors Ltd, 210 Old Steet, London EC1V 9UN.
- Two-Ten Communications, Communications House, 210 Old Street, London EC1V 9UN. Tel: 071 490 8111.
- Voice of America, 76 Shoe Lane, London EC4. Tel: 071 583 1452.

Other Useful Addresses

- Arts Council of Great Britain, 14 Great Peter Street, London SW1P 3NQ. Tel: 071 333 0100. Fax: 071 973 6590.
- British Copyright Council, Copyright House, 29–33 Berners Street, London W1P 4AA. Tel: 071 580 5544.
- British Council, Medlock Street, Manchester M15 4PR. Tel: 061 957 7000.
- British Council, Library, Books and Information Division, 10 Spring Gardens, London SW1A 2BN. Tel: 071 389 4886. Fax: 071 389 4949.
- Central Office of Information, Hercules Road, London SE1. Tel: 071 928 2345.
- Copyright Licensing Agency, 90 Tottenham Court Road, London W1P 9HE. Tel: 071 436 5931.
- DTI Export Publications, Box 55, Stratford-on-Avon, Warks CV37 9GE.
- EBSCO Subscription Services, 75 E Madison Avenue, Dumont, NJ 07628, USA.
- Export Credits Guarantees Division, PO Box 272, Export House, 50 Ludgate Hill, London EC4M 74Y. Tel: 071 512 7000.
- Kings Town Photocodes Limited, PO Box 15, Beverley, Yorks HU17 8DY. Tel: 0482 867321. Fax: 0482 882712.

- NERIS, Maryland College, Leighton Street, Woburn, MK17 9JD. Tel: 0525 290364. Fax: 0525 290288.
- Oxford Publicity Partnership, 36 Lonsdale Road, Summertown, Oxford OX2 7EW. Tel: 0865 53032. Fax: 0865 511489.
  Publicity services for small publishers.
- Point Eight, Shaw Road, Dudley, West Midlands DY2 8TP. Tel: 0384 258670.
- A T Smail, Copyright Libraries Agent, 100 Euston Street, London NW1 2QH. Tel: 071 388 506.
- Society of Authors, 84 Drayton Gardens, London SW10 9SD. Tel: 071 373 6642. Fax: 071 373 5768.
- UK Serials Group, 114 Woodstock Road, Witney, Oxon OX8 6DY. Tel: 0993 703466.

Glossary

This glossary concentrates primarily on the marketing terms used in publishing. To these we have added other terms that will be met in marketing but which are drawn from the related pursuits of editing, printing, binding and bookselling. Each entry below gives only one meaning unless the word 'also' is used. The glossary is confined to giving the specialist meanings of the words. Readers wanting a more detailed glossary of terms used by publishers, may care to refer to *Printing and Publishing Terms*, Martin H Manser (Chambers 1988).

advance information sheet/AI a promotion piece giving bibliographical details and a summary of a title. Produced between three and six months prior to publication, copies are mailed to library suppliers and key accounts and used by representatives to take orders in book shops. Usually A4 in size.

agent (1) a person or organisation representing several publishers to bookshops by soliciting orders which are returned to the publisher for servicing except in the case of a stock holding agent; also
  (2) an authors' or literary agent represents authors in their business dealings and in particular places manuscripts with publishers and other media.

artwork text and illustrations prepared for reproduction as *camera-ready copy*.

author questionnaire a specially prepared questionnaire for completion by authors and editors to provide marketing information for use by publishers.

author tour a tour by an author to bookshops and other venues to promote titles by readings, signings etc.

backlist the older titles on a publisher's list which are still in print; usually those published before the current season (spring or autumn) or in previous years.

bar code a machine-readable code incorporating a title's ISBN (and sometimes the selling price) printed on the back cover of books; see *electronic point of sale/EPoS*.

blurb the paragraphs found on leaflets, advertisements and book covers and jackets which tell the potential purchaser about the title.

book a non-periodical publication containing 49 or more pages, not counting the cover (UNESCO definition); more colloquially, a non-periodical publication produced with a spine. Compare with *pamphlet*.

book club a society which sells to its members/subscribers a limited range of books at less than the usual bookshop prices; usually specialist in orientation; members are committed to buying a specified number of titles per year. See Chapter 9.

bookseller a bookshop or anyone who works selling books in the retail or library trade.

break-even the point at which a publisher sells sufficient copies of a title to recoup the original costs of printing and production of that title.

buyer the person in a bookshop responsible for selecting and ordering from publishers; likely to be a shared responsibility between several people in a large shop.

camera-ready copy pages of text which are typeset, pasted-up and ready to go under the camera as the first stage in litho plate making for printing.

carriage the cost of shipping books from a distributor to a bookshop or other purchaser. Usually borne by the publisher in the UK market.

case-bound the binding of a hard-cover book.

cast off character count or word count of a typescript in order to assess its length when set in type and thus the extent of the publication.

character a letter, space, punctuation mark or symbol; see *cast off*.

CIF the abbreviation for cost, insurance and freight; used in exporting to mean that the seller pays the cost of freight and insurance to transport the books to the buyer's door. Compare with *FOB*.

closed market used of export markets meaning that a bookseller can only obtain a book from the publisher with exclusive rights in that territory, or from an official local agent; in other words that the market has been closed in favour of that publisher or agent. See also *open market*.

cloth the linen used to cover the boards of many hard-backs. Commonly used to describe a hard-cover book; many titles are catalogued as being available in cloth and paper editions, i.e. in hardback and paperback editions.

colophon a publisher's logo such as the bird on books published under the Penguin imprint.

commission a fee paid to an agent or representative for business executed; usually a percentage of invoice value. See also *discount*.

cooperative mailing a promotional mailing where two or more companies include leaflets in one envelope thus reducing costs.

copy words to be typeset; especially small pieces of text such as publicity pieces or newspaper articles.

copyright the exclusive legal right to reproduce literary or artistic property; usually governed by national copyright laws and by international conventions; in most instances copyright lies with the originator who then gives permission to publish the material. Denoted by the symbol ©.

counter pack a point-of-sale container produced by publishers for bookshops for the display of books.

cover now used almost entirely of paperbacks; compare *jacket*.

credit note a bill crediting a bookshop's account resulting from a shortage in delivery of invoiced goods or following the return of unsold, damaged or imperfect copies.

CTN an abbreviation for Confectioners, Tobacconists and Newagents.

delivery note often a copy of an invoice, this is a note sent with publications to a bookseller itemising titles, quantities, price, etc, of goods supplied; usually only used when invoices are being sent to a separate location; see also *invoice*.

desk top publishing/DTP a system incorporating a personal computer, appropriate software and a printer used to produce printed material to *camera-ready* standard.

direct costs costs of materials and services which are incurred on a specific title especially the printing and binding costs; see also *indirect costs* and *unit cost*.

discount the percentage off the retail price at which a publisher sells publications to a bookseller.

distributor a person or, more usually, an organisation that stocks books and services orders from bookshops on behalf of several publishers; distributors sometimes also have a team of representatives visiting bookshops in various parts of the country.

drawn-on cover a style of paperback binding where the cover is glued to the spine of the text.

dues orders placed with a publishers by booksellers for titles which are not immediately available; unless otherwise instructed, the publisher usually records the orders and supplies the titles when they become available.

dump bin a large free-standing container supplied by publishers for bookshops for the display of books; dump bins are usually made of cardboard and contain approximately 40–50 copies of a single title or a mixture of books by the same author or in a series.

edition one edition of a title is all the copies printed without alteration to the format or binding and without substantial alterations to text; one edition may consist of several impressions or printings.

educational contractor a firm which seeks contracts from Local Education Authorities or schools for the supply of books and educational materials.

embargo a time and date given on some press releases before which the resulting story should not appear in the press or other medium; this allows the publisher to give out information in advance of an event and should prevent a newspaper breaking a story earlier than others and destroying its news value for other newspapers.

EPoS an abbreviation for electronic point-of-sale systems; such systems usually incorporate computerised stock control and reorder generation triggered by scanning bar-codes at the moment of sale.

firm sale the usual form of sale where a bookseller orders books and does not expect to return any; UK publishers usually interpret this in a flexible manner and accept returns for credit if a bookseller requests to make them.

FOB an abbreviation for free-on-board; used in exporting to mean that the seller will be responsible for placing the books on a carrier at a specified place without extra charge; once delivered to the appropriate point, the goods become the responsibility of the purchaser. Compare with *CIF*.

format the physical characteristics of a publication, especially the shape and size but also the number of pages, type of binding, etc.

gross profit receipts from sales less direct expenditure on production; the major items not taken into account in calculating gross profit are overheads; contrast with *net profit*.

half-tone an illustration which reproduces the impression of the continuous tone of a photograph; a screen is used to achieve this effect by breaking the image into dots, i.e., the grey areas of a black and white photograph are broken into dots of black ink surrounded by white spaces which then look grey.

hardback a *case-bound* book; compare with *paperback*.

impression all copies of a publication printed at one time without altering the printing plates.

imprint the name under which a publishing house publishes a title (usually the name of the publishing house); some houses have several imprints, for instance, Random-Century publishes under the Chatto and Jonathan Cape imprints as well as various others.

indirect costs expenditure attributed to a title which is not included in direct costs; the main item is usually a percentage of overheads including office costs and salaries; see *direct costs*.

in-house work work which a publisher does within the organisation and does not place with outsiders.

insert promotional leaflet placed inside a periodical – can be bound in but is usually loose.

inspection copy a copy of a title sent to a lecturer or teacher for an approval period so that they can consider its suitability for class use. If recommended, the book can usually be kept free of charge but otherwise must be returned or purchased.

invoice a bill or note itemising the quantity, titles and retail prices of publications supplied against an order; shows discount applicable and a calculation of charges and reports reasons if certain titles are not supplied; usually sent with a parcel direct to booksellers, but see *delivery note*.

invoice value the amount shown on an invoice which the seller is charging; usually the sum of the retail price less the trade discount.

ISBN a ten digit number which uniquely identifies each publication or edition published; an abbreviation of International Standard Book Number.

ISSN an eight digit number used to identify a periodical; an abbreviation of International Standard Serial Number.

jacket, dustcover, wrapper printed paper covering placed round a cased/hardback book.

jobber (1) US term for a wholesaler/distributor; also
(2) used to describe a firm that deals in remainders.

journey order now somewhat archaic term to describe an order taken by a representative when visiting a bookshop.

laminated boards form of book covering where lamination is applied directly on to hardcover binding.

landscape the shape of a publication where the width exceeds the depth; the opposite, such as this guide, is called portrait.

layout a design showing the arrangement of type and illustrations on a page.

leaflet a publication consisting of a few, usually unstitched, pages without a cover of a different material.

library licence a licence issued by the Publishers Association allowing a bookseller to sell net books to a named library at a discount of not more than 10 per cent.

library supplier a firm specialising in supplying books to libraries.

limp form of book covering between cased and the normal paperback; usually card made to look like cloth; sometimes used to describe a robust, expensive and sewn paperback.

line work illustrations such as line drawings which contain no gradation of tone; compare with *half-tone;* cheaper to reproduce than photographs.

list all the titles a publisher has in print for sale; also used to mean the catalogue or printed list of a publisher's titles.

list broker a company supplying mailing lists for use in direct mail promotions.

list price, published price the retail price of a title fixed by the publisher (in countries where this is permitted) and usually printed in the publisher's catalogue.

mail shot a mailing of promotional pieces to potential purchasers.

marketing activities planned and executed to ensure that a publication or range of publications is purchased by as many people or organisations as possible from as many points of sale as is desired; often taken to include promotion, sales and distribution activities.

mark-up (1) to prepare manuscript for the typesetter by writing on instructions;
   (2) to increase the price of a title above the list price; sometimes necessary when a new publisher has allowed insufficient margin in their costing to give a realistic discount or when selling expenses are high, as in exporting; also
   (3) used by importers of books when setting UK market prices and meaning the amount by which a price has been increased above the par exchange rate of the currency in question.

minimum order the minimum number of units a bookseller may order from a publisher; usually only used by the larger houses.

net book a book that must not be sold to the public at less than the list price in the UK; see *non net*.

Net Book Agreement an agreement between publishers and booksellers which governs the retail prices of books within the UK. See Chapter 5.

net profit any surplus that remains after all the costs of production and overheads have been deducted from the gross income received.

net receipts the money received by a publisher on sale of publications, less selling costs such as freight or postage.

non-net book a book that may be sold to the public by a bookseller at less than the price recommended by the publisher; usually a book aimed at the school market.

not known a report made to a bookseller by a publisher or distributor to indicate that a title ordered is not their publication; abbreviated to N/K.

not yet published title still in the stages of production; abbreviated to NYP.

on-costs the general office costs, eg, light, heat and rent, that may be shared amongst publications rather than being allocated to any one particular production.

open market territories where more than one edition of a title may be sold, without restrictions, by agreement between publishers; see *closed market*.

origination the stages involved in preparing a manuscript for printing; this covers editing, typesetting and illustrations.

out-of-print title no longer available from publisher and for which no reprint is envisaged; abbreviated to O/P.

out-of-stock not currently available but new stock is planned (do not confuse with *out-of-print*); abbreviated to O/S.

overheads in publishing these are usually considered to be salaries, rent, office expenses, and other expenses not relating to the production of publications, such as promotion.

page this entry is on one page; taken together with its other side they make a leaf or taken together with its facing page they make a double page spread.

pamphlet a non-periodical publication with fewer than 49 pages but more than eight (UNESCO definition); a small publication without a spine often educational, ephemeral or polemical.

paperback a book with a spine and usually paper or card covers; usually *perfect bound*.

perfect binding a process by which the back folds of *signatures* are trimmed flush and the resulting pages glued to the inside of the spine of the cover; this is more expensive than stapling but cheaper than sewing; used extensively for paperbacks.

point of sale display material placed in book shops used to draw customers' attention to particular titles, for example a *counter pack*.

prelims the pages preceding the text of a publication; often paginated in Roman numerals.

press release an anouncement sent to the press telling them of an event or news item.

print run the number of copies of a title printed at one printing.

production ledger a publisher's record of expenditure incurred publishing a title; compile this as you incur the expenses and check against your estimate and proposed selling price.

pro-forma invoice an invoice that must be paid by the bookseller before the publisher will dispatch the book(s); usually used when the bookseller does not have an account with the publisher.

promotion activities designed to publicise a list or publication usually around publication date; these may include mailing review copies, leaflets and press releases; most promotion is done to create demand amongst potential readers but some will be aimed at booksellers and library suppliers.

publication date the official date of publication fixed by a publisher for a title, before which bookshops should not sell it nor the media review it; these dates are now widely ignored by the trade and the media but still used by publishers to enable promotion to be concentrated around one date.

published price see *list price*.

rate card a data card containing rates for advertising in a periodical.

reading a promotional event where an author reads to the public from his or her book.

recto a right hand page or front of a leaf. The opposite of *verso*.

remainder to sell off overstocks at a reduced price; a move usually initiated by the publisher when sales of a title have fallen to such a level that it is uneconomic to keep it in print.

representative a person who visits bookshops to sell publications and take orders; he or she might work for publishers, a firm of representatives or as a freelance; often abbreviated to 'rep'.

reprint to print a second or subsequent impression of a title.

reprinting a report given on a publisher's invoice to indicate that a book is of stock but is being reprinted; abbreviated as R/P.

review copy a copy of a publication sent to the media before publication so that reviews can be written to appear around the publication date.

review list/plan the list of people to whom review copies will be sent.

review slip a note enclosed with a review copy giving price, publication date and other bibliographical details and sometimes a summary of the publication and a note on the author(s).

rights the legal authority to publish a work; permission given by the copyright holder in the first instance, to reproduce a work in one of the various forms such as paperback rights, serial rights and film rights.

royalty percentage of list price or net receipt paid to the author/editor/illustrator on each copy sold.

saddle-stitching binding by means of wire staples (or thread) through the fold; the most common form of binding pamphlets.

sale or return a publisher's or distributor's term which is interpreted in various ways; usually publications are left with a bookseller and after a specified period unsold copies are taken back and payment made for the copies sold; used frequently for magazines but not recommended for other publications except when the bookseller has arranged to hold extra stock for a special promotion such as a major window display. Compare with *see safe*.

sanserif, sans-serif type without finishing strokes at the end of a line or bar of a letter or character; as used for tables and figures in this book.

see safe publications supplied and charged to a bookseller with the agreement that they may be returned for credit or in exchange for other books if they do not sell.

serif finishing stroke at the end of a line or bar of a letter or character; the text of this book is set in a serif face.

ship to release copies of a new title to the trade (US).

signature a folded printed sheet, usually comprising 16 or 32 pages.

signing session an arranged visit to a bookshop or other venue by an author to sign copies of his or her book for sale to the public.

single-copy single-line an order for one copy of one title on which publishers often give a short discount or levy a service charge.

sleeper a title that is slow to sell initially but later takes off (US); also a name inserted in a mailing list to ensure that this list has only been used once if purchased on that condition.

specifications the production details of a publication, for example the number of pages, format, type of paper, binding etc; sent to printer to obtain quotes.

spinner a revolving display unit used by publishers to display their titles in bookshops.

statement a summary of the invoices and credit notes issued to a purchaser and the payments received over a specified period (usually a month); indicates what payments are due and the net balance outstanding.

subscribe to secure order from booksellers for a publication prior to the publication date; a very important form of raising orders.

teleorder an electronic system employed by booksellers to forward orders to publishers and distributors via a central computer.

terms the discount and credit period offered by a publisher to a bookseller; terms may vary with types of publication, size of order and nature of the outlet.

title separate publications on a publisher's list; you are currently reading one copy of one title; also used to mean the name of a book.

trade counter a place from which booksellers can collect copies of a publisher's books; usually more central than the warehouse.

trade terms see *terms*.

turnover the sum of the invoice value of orders invoiced over a specified period, usually a year, less any credits issued; note that not all the cash will have been received, some will not be due until the next year.

unit cost the cost of producing a title divided by the number of copies printed; some publishers include *indirect costs* or an element of *on-costs* as well as *direct costs*.

verso a left hand page or the back of a leaf as in the verso of the title page; see *recto*.

wholesaler company buying books in bulk from a publisher for sale to retailers.

Bibliography

This is a select bibliography of books on publishing and the book industry. Titles listed here are not necessarily all currently available but are included in Whitaker's or American *Books in Print* at the time of writing unless otherwise indicated. Not all have been consulted in the preparation of this book.

With a few exceptions, it is restricted to books published since 1980. Latest editions are listed, although of course many of the directories and yearbooks are revised annually.

American Book Trade Directory (annual). Bowker, USA
Bar Coding for Books: A Guide for Publishers (1992). Book Industry Communications
Baverstock, A (1990) *How to Market Books*. Kogan Page
Book Buying by Commercial and Industrial Libraries (1985). Publishers Association
Book Distribution: A Handbook for Booksellers and Publishers in the UK (1988). Blueprint Publishers
Book Marketing Handbook (1980/83) 2 volumes. Bowker, USA
Book Marketing News. Publishers Association
Book Prices in the UK (1989). British National Bibliographic Research Fund
Book Printing in Britain and the USA: A Guide to the Literature and a Directory of Printers (1983). Greenwood Press
Book Production Practice (1978). Publishers Association/British Federation of Master Printers
Book Publishers' Representatives Handbook (1989). Book Publishers' Representatives Association
Book Publishing in the United Kingdom: Key Facts 1981–88 (1989). Publishers Association
Book Publishing: What it is, What it does (1981). Bowker, USA (2nd edn)
Book Trade of the World, 4 volumes. K G Saur
The Bookseller. J Whitaker
Booksellers Association Charter Group Economic Survey (annual). Booksellers Association
Booksellers Association List of Members (annual). Booksellers Association
Also available are specialist group lists: Children's Booksellers, College and University Booksellers, Export Booksellers, Library Booksellers, Religious Booksellers, School Suppliers and Wholesalers.
Brinton, W M (1987) *A Role for the Small Press: Publishing in a Global Village*. Mercury House, San Francisco

British Book News. British Council

British Code of Sales Promotion Practice (1980). Code of Advertising Practice Committee (3rd edn)

British Exporting Booksellers (1990). British Council

British National Bibliography. British Library

Butcher, J. *Copy-editing: The Cambridge Handbook* (1983). Cambridge University Press

Cavendish, J (1984) *Handbook of Copyright in British Publishing Practice*. Cassell (2nd edn)

Clark, C (1988) *Publishing Agreements: A Book of Precedents*. Unwin Hyman (3rd edn)

Clark, G N (1988*) Inside Book Publishing: A Career Builder's Guide*. Blueprint

Code of Practice: Guidelines for Publishers and their Relations with Authors (1982). Publishers Association

Customs of the Trade for the Manufacture of Books (1979). Publishers Association

Dalton, A-M (1991) *The Arts Funding Guide*, Directory of Social Change (2nd edn)

Direct Marketing Services (1988). Benn Business Information Services

Directory of Book Publishers, Distributors and Wholesalers (annual). Booksellers Association

Directory of Publishing (annual). Cassell and the Publishers Association

Directory of Small Presses (annual). Dustbooks, USA

Directory of Specialist Bookdealers in the United Kingdom (1988). P Marcan (4th edn)

Do-It-Yourself – Self Publishing and Book Promotion (1990). Artmusique Publishing Co.

Euromonitor Book Report (1991). Euromonitor

European Bookseller. European Bookseller, London

Foster, C, *Editing, Design and Book Production* (in prep.). Journeyman

Glossary of Book Trade Terminology (1989). Publishers Association (7th edn)

Guide to Literary Prizes, Grants and Awards (1988). Book Trust/Society of Authors (5th edn)

Henderson, B (ed) (1987) T*he Publish-It-Yourself Handbook: Literary Tradition and How-To*. Pushcart Press, USA (3rd edn)

Hughes, V M (1991) *Literature Belongs to Everyone*. Arts Council

Jacob, H (1976) *Pocket Dictionary of Publishing Terms*. MacDonald

Knight, J, (1988) *Book Publishing*. Media

Legat, M, (1982) *An Author's Guide to Publishing*. Robert Hale

Library Book Selling: A Survey of the Costs of Processing by Booksellers (1979). Booksellers Association

Making the Connections: Radical Books Today (1988). Federation of Radical Booksellers

Mann, P H (1979) *Book Publishing, Book Selling and Book Reading*. Publishers Association

Manser, M H (1988) *Printing and Publishing Terms*. Chambers

Marketing Electronic Publications (1987). Publishers Association

Mumby, F A and Norrie, I (1984) *Publishing and Bookselling*. Bell and Hyman (6th edn)

Owen, L (1991) *Selling Rights: A Publisher's Guide to Success*. Blueprint

Owen, P (ed) (1988) *Publishing: The Future*. Peter Owen

Page, G et al (1987) *Journal Publishing: Principles and Practice*. Butterworth

Poynter, D (1989) *The Self-Publishing Manual: How to Write, Print and Sell your own Book*. Parachuting Publications, USA (5th edn)

Print Production Manual (1988). Blueprint Publishing (3rd edn)

Publishers in the United Kingdom and their Addresses (annual). Whitaker

Publishers Trade List Annual, 6 volumes. Bowker, USA

Publishers Weekly. Bowker, USA. (The US equivalent of *The Bookseller*.)

Quillam and Stephenson, *Into Print* (1990). BBC Books

Radical Bookseller. Federation of Radical Booksellers (irregular)

The Radical Bookshop Guide (1988). Federation of Radical Booksellers

Small Press Record of Books in Print (1989). Dustbooks, USA

Small Press Yearbook (annual). Small Press Group of Britain

The State of Reading: on the role of books in schools today. Publishers Association

Ulrich's International Periodicals Directory (annual). Bowker, USA

Unwin, S (1976) *The Truth About Publishing*. Unwin Hyman (8th edn)

Ward, A and Ward, P (1979) *The Small Publisher: A Manual and Case Histories*. Oleander Press

Ward, S (1992) *Getting the Message Across: Public Relations, Publicity and Working with the Media*. Journeyman

West, C and Wheat, V (1978/80) *The Passionate Perils of Publishing*, 2 volumes. Bootlegger Press, USA

Whitaker's Books in Print (annual, non-book editions updated monthly). J Whitaker

Women in Publishing (ed) (1987) *Reviewing the Reviews: A Woman's Place on the Book Page*. Journeyman

Wren, J (ed) (1990) *Guide to Women Book Publishers in the United States*. Clothespin Fever Press, USA (2nd edn)

Writers' and Artists' Yearbook (annual). A & C Black

Zeitlin, J, *Effective Publicity and Design* (1992). Journeyman

Titles published by the Publishers Association are available from them at the address given in the address section of this book. The Book Trust also publish a number of titles on book buying and reading patterns in the British Isles. Blueprint publish many titles on the publishing and printing industries.

The Post Office frequently publish free guides to effective direct mail and to their discount arrangements for bulk mailings. Contact the Marketing Department, Postal Headquarters, St Martins-le-Grand, London EC1A 1HQ.

Index